Questions and Answers
INVENTIONS

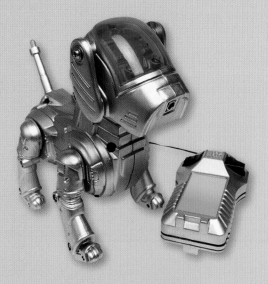

Author: Louise Spilsbury
Consultant: Chris Cooper
Editor: Jane Yorke
Design by: Chris Scollen and Macwiz

First published by Parragon in 2007

Parragon
Queen Street House
4 Queen Street
Bath BA1 1HE, UK

ISBN 978-1-4054-9462-5

Printed in China

Questions and Answers
INVENTIONS

HOW? WHY? WHERE? WHEN?

Bath · New York · Singapore · Hong Kong · Cologne · Delhi · Melbourne

CONTENTS

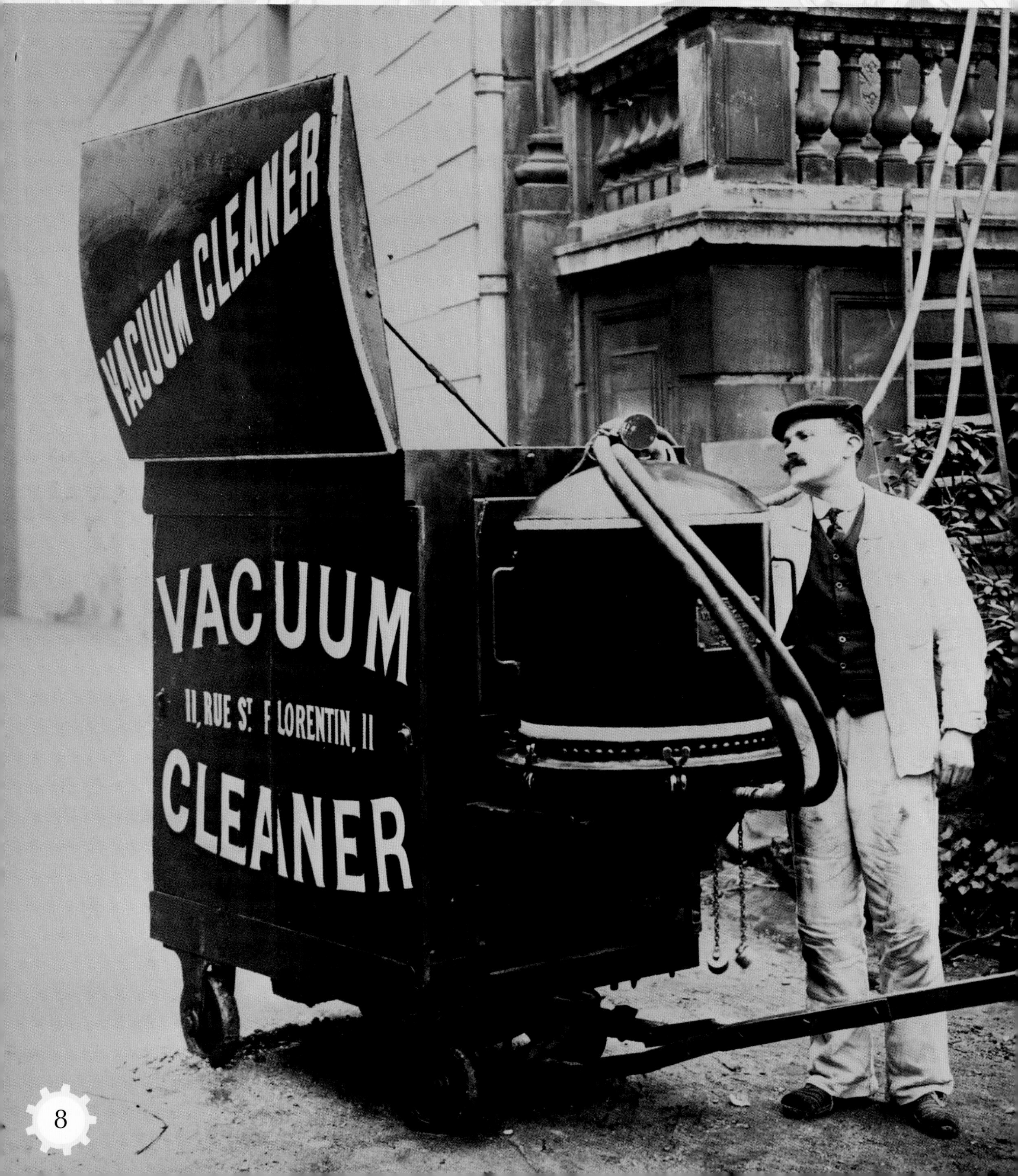
VACUUM CLEANER
VACUUM
11, RUE St. FLORENTIN, 11
CLEANER

INVENTIONS

Our lives would be a lot more difficult and probably less fun without inventions. Find out what an inventions is, why people invent things, and when most inventions were created. Learn about patents and why some worked while others didn't. Discover how inventions might change our lives in the future.

WHAT IS AN INVENTION?

What is an invention?

An invention is a new object, like a spring, or a new material, such as nylon, or a process, like freezing food. When something is discovered it needs an invention to make it useful. People discovered fire over a million years ago when lightning caused natural fires. But they couldn't control fire until they had invented a way of making it by rubbing sticks together or striking flints. Matches weren't invented until AD 577 in China.

BELOW Everything made by people has an inventor, the person who came up with the idea for it in the first place.

catapult

mouse trap

Slinky toy invented in 1945

BELOW The first vacuum cleaners were so big that they were taken door to door for rent.

Why do people invent things?

People usually invent things to make life easier. Household appliances, such as the vacuum cleaner, have revolutionized housework. Most inventions develop from earlier ideas. For example, in 250 BC, a Greek inventor called Archimedes explained how levers worked. This led to many other inventions including scissors, nutcrackers, and tweezers. Sometimes, a new invention is an improvement on an old one, such as the vacuum cleaner. But some inventions are made by accident. The Slinky toy was developed when some springs fell off a work bench. Silly Putty was invented while someone was trying to make a material to replace rubber. And Teflon, the nonstick coating used on saucepans, was the result of a mistake by its inventor, scientist Roy Plunkett.

When were most inventions made?

People have always had great ideas but haven't always had the materials or technology to make them happen. In the last 250 years, the discovery of electricity, new chemical materials, and advances in microbiology have led to an explosion of inventions. Today, large companies, universities, and governments have research laboratories to develop new inventions.

ABOVE Albert Einstein didn't invent anything, but made many major scientific discoveries that led to countless modern inventions, such as nuclear energy, lasers, and microchips.

RIGHT Leonardo da Vinci drew up plans for a submarine in the 15th century, 400 years before the first submarine went to war.

What is a patent?

A patent is a way for inventors to protect their ideas. When an inventor has a new idea, the can government grant a patent to the inventor. The patent gives the inventor the legal right, for a fixed period of time, to stop other people from making, using, or selling the invention except with the inventor's permission. Many more inventions are patented than ever succeed. Trademarks also protect the name of an invention. Trademarks tell us the source of a product or service and give us information about quality and consistency. Trademarks have been found on pottery made in around 5000 BC.

RIGHT Inventor Dean Kamem filed a patent for the Segway Human Transporter in 1999. No one knows whether this invention will become a household name.

THE FUTURE OF INVENTIONS

Every single thing around us—the shoes we wear, the chairs we sit on, the glass in the windows, the ball we kick and throw, this book itself—was invented in the past. The inventions here are a sample of some we might see in the future. However strange and unbelievable they may seem, remember that this is what people in the past thought of ideas like the automobile and the airplane, which we now take for granted.

What will we drive in the future?

In the future, we won't be driving cars—computers will. Computerized cars and highways will do the work while drivers sleep or read. In-car cameras could watch white line markings and keep vehicles in their lanes and computers in cars could judge distances for parking, using laser, ultrasonics, or radar. And, at the end of a trip, the automatic car park will drop vehicles into parking lots and retrieve them on demand!

ABOVE Cameras on the dashboard of an interactive car feed information about road markings and signs to an onboard computer.

How will robots make us better?

In the future, scientists hope to be able to build microscopic machines, measuring just millionths of a millimeter. These nanobots will travel inside the human body to help make us better. Medical scientists say that, using this nanotechnology, machines will be able to venture through blood vessels, like tiny robot doctors, cleaning them or destroying cancer cells.

LEFT A nanobot searches for cancer cells in the blood.

Will we still have to do housework?

In homes of the future, household chores may be a thing of the past! Computer networks will link smart home appliances such as cookers and fridges. These will have sensors and microchips so that cookers will turn on and off automatically and your fridge will alert you when food is about to go bad. We'll be able to program our homes using a remote control unit or even a cell phone from miles away.

When will we vacation in space?

Who knows—within 50 years there might be a "highway to space" that will enable us to travel, work, and live in space. In future, space transportation will probably be linked with international airport systems, so we will see planes flying to New York City from the same runway as another leaving for the Moon.

ABOVE The Wakamaru robot, made by Mitsubishi, is a companion that can have simple conversations and report to a control center if something's wrong in the house. It went on sale in 2005.

NASA 1 X-43A

LEFT NASA is working on an aircraft that will revolutionize space travel.

FARMING

From stone plows to powerful combine harvesters, inventions have helped us to grow and prepare food. Find out how milking machines work, and what irrigation devices farmers use to water their crops. Learn about why canning and freezing helps preserve foods and how insecticides get rid of crop pests. Discover what GM food means, and why we might one day be eating purple carrots.

FARMING KEY DATES

| **6000 BC** First stone hand tools for farming | **3500 BC** Ox-drawn plow invented | **2500 BC** Shaduf used to collect water | **260 BC** Archimedes' screw used for irrigation | **AD 1810** Metal can invented for preserving food |

PLOWS

What were the first farm tools?

Around 6000 BC, farmers in the Middle East invented a simple tool, called an adze, for digging and hoeing the soil. This had a wooden handle tied to a pointed stone head. The earliest sickles were made with flint. This stone could be chipped to make a sharp edge for cutting down tall crops, such as wheat, in the fields.

adze

sickle

Why were plows invented?

Farmers soon learned that seeds grow best in broken-up soil. But it was hard work digging the fields using hand tools. So around 5000 BC, farmers invented the plow to help them. The first plows were pulled along by people. They consisted of a simple wooden frame attached to an upright digging stick. This was dragged through the soil to make small trenches, or furrows, in the field.

DID YOU KNOW?
The first farmers to use oxen to pull plows were the Sumerians of Mesopotamia over 5,000 years ago. The pulling power of the animals took the hard work out of plowing.

BELOW John Deere's steel walking plow was pulled by a horse.

When were iron plows made?

The trouble with wooden plows was that they wore out quickly. Around 3000 years ago, people discovered how to make iron tools. By 900 BC, farmers were making sharp and long-lasting tips for their plows out of iron. By 500 BC, plows were made completely from iron. In 1838, American blacksmith John Deere invented the first ever, cast-steel plow.

How do plows work?

Modern plows have curved blades called mold boards. These dig a furrow by turning over the ground, burying weeds and adding air to the soil. When the pulling tractor turns in the field, the plow rotates so that the resting blades, which curve the other way, can be used.

BELOW A sharp blade, called a coulter, breaks up the soil before the plow blades move through it.

resting blades

mold board   plowing blade   coulter

17

FARMING KEY DATES

6000 BC First stone hand tools for farming	**3500 BC** Ox-drawn plow invented	**2500 BC** Shaduf used to collect water	**260 BC** Archimedes' screw used for irrigation	**AD 1810** Metal can invented for preserving food

TRACTORS

When were tractors invented?

In the 19th century, farmers started to use traction engines to operate farm machines. These heavy engines used steam power to do the work of people or animals. However, early traction engines were expensive to run and too heavy to pull farm machinery over rough or soft ground. In 1892, American John Froehlich built the first practical tractor with an engine that ran on gasoline.

BELOW a steam-powered traction engine

Large, grooved tires provide grip on rough ground.

LEFT An open-air tractor harvesting hay.

The three-point hitch is used for attaching farm machinery.

What are tractors used for today?

Today's powerful tractors are comfortable to drive and can pull trailers piled high with heavy loads and power different kinds of farm machinery. They drag plows to dig fields, giant rakes, called harrows, to break up the soil, and seed drills to plant seeds in straight rows. Using a tractor makes farm work quicker and easier for farmers.

Who invented the combine harvester?

In the early 20th century, tractors were often used at harvesttime to reap, or cut down, cereal crops such as wheat. Separate threshing machines were needed to separate the grains from the stalks. In 1938, the Canadian company, Massey-Harris, sold its combine harvester to farmers for the first time. The machine had an engine to power itself along and it could both reap and thresh the crop, so that farmers could harvest larger areas in a faster time.

BELOW The huge cutters on a combine harvester cut down wide strips of crops.

The powerful engine pulls heavy loads and also drives machinery.

Why do tractors have big wheels?

Most tractors have two small wheels in the front and two huge driving wheels in the back, which are powered by the engine. At first, tractors had spiked metal wheels, but in the 1930s, inflatable tractor tires were invented. These helped tractors move on soft, muddy ground. They also helped to spread the tractor's weight to stop it from sinking.

DID YOU KNOW?
Some tractors don't have tires, but run on rubber caterpillar tracks instead. The tracks have ridges to provide grip on both rough and soft ground.

A glass cab allows the farmer to see all around when operating machinery.

The front and back wheels steer separately so that the tractor can turn in very small spaces.

FARMING KEY DATES

| 6000 BC First stone hand tools for farming | 3500 BC Ox-drawn plow invented | 2500 BC Shaduf used to collect water | 260 BC Archimedes' screw used for irrigation | AD 1810 Metal can invented for preserving food |

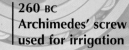

DAIRY MACHINES

When was the milking machine invented?

Milking a herd of cows by hand was a long, hard job before American engineer L. O. Colvin patented his time-saving milking machine in 1860. The farmer attached rubber cups to a cow's teats and then pumped on some bellows. This sucked milk out of the udder through hoses into a bucket. But the machine sucked milk constantly, which often damaged the cow's teats.

How do milking machines work?

Today's dairy farmers use automated milking machines. These can milk a large herd of about 100 cows in a couple of hours. In the milking shed, the farmer first washes the cow's four teats and then attaches the milking cups. The machine's vacuum pump gently sucks the teats in an on-off motion. This draws the milk from the udder in the same way that a calf does.

Milking cups are attached to the teats on each cow's udder.

RIGHT The milk from each cow runs along pipes into jars, where it is measured. Then the milk is pumped into a large cooling tank. It is stored here until it is collected by tanker and taken to the milk processor.

Who invented cheese?

People have been using milk to produce cheese for over 5,000 years. Cheese was probably invented by nomads in the Middle East, who traveled with their goat and sheep herds looking for fresh pasture. The story goes that a nomad once stored milk in a saddlebag made from a sheep's stomach. Warmed by the sun, the milk mixed with the rennet in the animal's stomach and formed curdled lumps—the first cheese.

The curd is chopped and mixed with salt to form cheese.

BELOW When milk is warmed and mixed with rennet it forms lumps of curd and watery whey.

The whey is drained off.

Weigh jars record how much milk each cow produces.

What is pasteurized milk?

Pasteurization is the process of heating food to destroy the harmful bacteria in it and make it safe to eat. The process is named after its inventor, French chemist Louis Pasteur, who first tested it on milk in 1862. Most milk today is pasteurized by being quickly heated to 162° Fahrenheit. This kills any bacteria that are in the milk and helps keep it fresh for longer.

DID YOU KNOW?
Robotic milking sheds allow cows to go in to be milked at any time. Computers trigger the removal of the milking cups when a cow's udders are empty.

21

FARMING KEY DATES

6000 BC	3500 BC	2500 BC	260 BC	AD 1810
First stone hand	Ox-drawn plow	Shaduf used to	Archimedes' screw	Metal can invented
tools for farming	invented	collect water	used for irrigation	for preserving food

CROP WATERING

Why do farmers water their crops?

Plants, like all living things, need water to live and grow. In places with plenty of rain, crops naturally get the water they need. In countries of the world that are drier, or during times of low rainfall, many crops can only grow if they are watered by people. The different methods farmers use to water their crops are called irrigation.

DID YOU KNOW?
Some farmers use a computerized system of moisture sensors to check how dry the soil is. Then at the press of a few buttons, they can drip-feed more water to their crops.

When was the shaduf invented?

The shaduf is a simple machine invented in ancient Egypt in around 2500 BC. It is still used to help people collect water from rivers today. The shaduf has a long pole balanced on a pivot. It has a bucket at one end and a heavy rock at the other to act as a counterweight. The bucket is first pulled down into the river and filled with water. Then the load is easily lifted up by the weight of the rock pulling down on the pole.

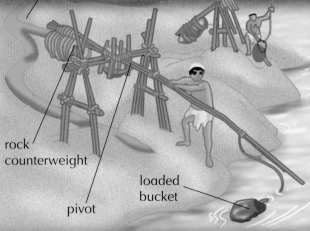

The water is poured into ditches and carried to nearby fields.

rock counterweight

pivot

loaded bucket

HOW does the Archimedes' screw work?

The Archimedes' screw is an early type of pump still used in some places to raise water for irrigation. It was first written about by the Greek engineer Archimedes in around 260 BC. The machine has a hollow tube with a tight-fitting screw inside. One end of the machine is dipped in the river and scoops up water as the screw is turned. Water travels to the top of the tube, where it runs out into an irrigation ditch.

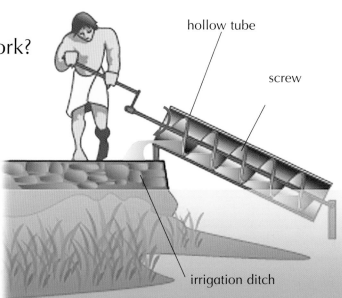

hollow tube

screw

irrigation ditch

BELOW A circular field is watered with a long sprinkler arm on wheels, which turns like the hands of a clock.

What do modern farmers use for irrigation?

Today, many farmers use a system of electric pumps, pipes, and sprinklers to move water from rivers and reservoirs to their crops. Pivot irrigation uses motors or water pressure in the pipes to move spray arms in a circle, so that all areas of a field are watered. However, water spray can quickly evaporate from plants in the hot sun. Drip irrigation uses holes in pipes, laid on or in the ground, to get water directly to the crop roots.

FARMING KEY DATES

| 6000 BC First stone hand tools for farming | 3500 BC Ox-drawn plow invented | 2500 BC Shaduf used to collect water | 260 BC Archimedes' screw used for irrigation | AD 1810 Metal can invented for preserving food |

FARM CHEMICALS

Why do farmers use chemicals?

Many crop farmers use chemical pesticides and fertilizers to help increase the amount of food they can grow. Fertilizers add nutrients to the soil, helping plants to grow bigger and produce more leaves or fruit. Pesticides include insecticides that remove insect pests, herbicides that kill weeds, and fungicides, which are sprayed on crops to prevent plant diseases or molds.

ABOVE Farmers rent small planes called "cropdusters" to spray pesticides over large fields. By spraying pesticides from a plane, the operator is safely out of the way of the chemicals.

BELOW Farmers wear protective clothing when spraying herbicides by hand.

What were the first insecticides?

Insecticides are chemical sprays used by farmers to repel or kill the insect pests that eat their crops. People have used natural substances to get rid of insects since ancient times. Some bug destroyers of the past include salt, tobacco, red pepper, and poisonous arsenic. In 1939, Swiss chemist Paul Müller discovered that a chemical called DDT made a good insecticide. Since then, a great many chemical insecticides have been produced and sold.

LEFT Some crop pests, such as this blister beetle, spoil plants by eating their leaves. Others feed on roots or suck sap from

When are farm chemicals harmful?

In some parts of the world, farmers use huge amounts of chemicals, which is not good for the natural environment. Some of these pesticides and fertilizers harm or even kill plants and harmless animals, such as rare wildflowers or butterflies. When the chemicals wash into the soil and rivers they can pollute them. And chemical traces left on crops, such as lettuce or fruit, can make people sick, if they eat too many of them.

Nozzles on the underside of the plane release even amounts of the chemicals in a fine spray.

DID YOU KNOW?
As long ago as 4500 BC, farmers in Mesopotamia burned sulfer from nearby volcanoes. The stinky smoke kept insect pests off their crops.

How do organic farmers grow crops?

BELOW Farmers check their fields throughout the growing season for signs of pest damage.

Organic farmers grow crops without using artificial chemicals. They use compost and manure from farm animals in place of artificial fertilizers. These farmers also encourage wildflowers to grow in their herbicide-free fields. Some flowers attract helpful insects, which eat the crop-destroying bugs. Organic farmers can also deter pests by growing smelly plants, like garlic, or spraying natural insecticides, such as the bitter-tasting oil from the tropical neem tree.

25

FARMING KEY DATES

| **6000 BC** First stone hand tools for farming | **3500 BC** Ox-drawn plow invented | **2500 BC** Shaduf used to collect water | **260 BC** Archimedes' screw used for irrigation | **AD 1810** Metal can invented for preserving food |

GM FOODS

What is GM food?

GM stands for "genetically modified". GM food comes from plants or animals that have had their genes altered by scientists. Genes are the inherited chemical "instructions" found in all living cells that make plants and animals the way they are. Scientists can now alter food plants by removing or adding extra genes to create new crops that stay fresh longer, are not spoiled by pesticides, or can grow in dry soils.

LEFT GM peaches are disease-resistant.

DID YOU KNOW?
GM scientists have created purple carrots and orange cauliflowers that contain around 25 times more vitamins than the usual kinds. These vegetables would certainly make dinnertime more colorful!

BELOW Some GM sunflowers produce a healthier type of oil.

When were GM foods invented?

The first GM food plant went on sale in 1994. The "Flavr Savr" tomato contained an altered gene to keep it firm and fresh for longer. Most tomatoes are picked when green and ripened later. The modified tomatoes were picked when red and did not go soft during transportation. They tasted better than ordinary tomatoes because they were ripened on the plant.

How are plants genetically modified?

Scientists can shoot new genes directly into plant cells using a special kind of gun. Next, the cells are put into a liquid, which helps them grow into whole plants. Scientists can also add new genes to bacteria, which then infect plant cells and modify its genes. This is how a frost-resistant gene from a fish was put into a tomato plant. The result was tomato fruits that are not damaged by cold weather.

LEFT Scientists monitor their GM experiments by growing modified plants in greenhouses.

GM protesters worry that GM crops are not safe in the environment. They fear that GM crops might cross-breed with normal crops growing in nearby fields.

BELOW GM wheat is not damaged by herbicides.

Who knows if GM crops are safe to eat?

Some people are concerned that genetic modification could be harmful to human health. They say that scientists don't fully understand how genes work and that altering plant genes could create foods that are poisonous or cause allergies. GM scientists and supporters say that no one eating GM foods has yet become sick and GM crops are needed to help farmers grow enough food to feed all the people on Earth.

FARMING KEY DATES

6000 BC	3500 BC	2500 BC	260 BC	AD 1810
First stone hand tools for farming	Ox-drawn plow invented	Shaduf used to collect water	Archimedes' screw used for irrigation	Metal can invented for preserving food

PRESERVING FOOD

Why do people preserve food?

Bacteria in the air feed on fresh food, such as fruit and vegetables. This makes them discolor quickly and rot. By packing fresh food in lidded jars under oil or pickling foods in vinegar, people discovered they could stop bacteria from spoiling food. In this way, people were able to enjoy summer foods in the cold months of winter, long before canning and freezing were invented.

ABOVE Fresh fruits, like these peaches, can be preserved in syrup and stored in airtight jars.

BELOW Today, fresh fish is caught, prepared, packed, and frozen at sea on huge factory ships.

bridge

cargo storage area

Fish are caught in a large net and dragged on board.

The fish are gutted and cut into fillets by machine.

The fillets are sorted, packed, and then quickly frozen on large, flat plate freezers, all within hours of being caught.

How is food quick-frozen?

The freezing process works by blasting food with a stream of very cold air, which quickly turns all the water inside it into small ice crystals. The very low temperatures stop harmful bacteria from growing. Many foods are also rapidly heated up before freezing. This stops the natural activity of enzymes in food, which can change its taste and appearance.

DID YOU KNOW?
X-rays passed through food can kill germs to stop it from getting moldy. Astronauts eat food treated by irradiation like this to keep from getting food poisoning in space.

Who invented the tin can?

Englishman Peter Durand invented metal cans for preserving food in 1810. He recognized that while food heated in a sealed, airtight can would keep for longer, the steel from the can would rust and spoil the food inside. Durand solved this problem by lining the steel cans with tin, which does not rust. Canned food quickly became popular with soldiers and sailors on long trips away from home.

BELOW The first can openers punctured the can and sliced it open with a blade.

crew cabins

The fish waste is turned into fish meal to feed farm animals.

BELOW Frozen fish went on sale for the first time in 1922. It was quick-frozen using the process developed by the American Clarence Birdseye.

When was the can opener invented?

Early tin cans were so solid they could only be opened using a hammer and chisel! Almost fifty years later, the first can opener was invented by the American Ezra Warner in 1858, when cans started to be made with thinner metal. It had a sharp blade that was pushed into the lid of the can to cut around the rim and force it open.

BUILDING

Modern machines, like giant excavators and bulldozers, make building houses, roads, bridges, and skyscrapers possible. But discover which small, simple tool the ancient Egyptians used to create their perfect pyramids, and why oven-baked bricks are still used today. Read about the giant steel skeletons that hold up the world's tallest skyscrapers. Find out how glass is made and what a spaghetti junction is.

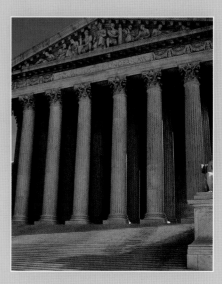

BUILDING KEY DATES

4000 BC	3500 BC	2000 BC	700 BC	AD 100
First canals	First oven-baked	Clapper bridges	First aqueduct built	Lifting machines first
in use	clay bricks	used to cross rivers	to carry water	used for building

BUILDING MATERIALS

BELOW Ziggurat temples were built in the shape of a stepped pyramid.

Who made the first bricks?

Prehistoric tribes made the first bricks by mixing mud and straw into blocks and leaving them to dry in the sun. This makes bricks the oldest manufactured building material. The first oven-baked clay bricks were made in 3500 BC, in Mesopotamia. These were used to build the first cities and ziggurat temples. Clay bricks are still used in buildings around the world today.

LEFT A special truck turns wet concrete inside a big drum so that it does not set until it is delivered.

Why was concrete invented?

Concrete can hold huge weights. In 1756, British engineer John Smeaton made the first modern concrete by mixing pebbles and powdered brick with a cement powder and water. When wet, concrete is poured into a mold and then left to dry hard. Concrete is a tough building material, but it cracks if bent or stretched. After 1867, steel rods were set inside concrete to give it extra strength.

DID YOU KNOW?
The Masai tribe in Africa build their traditonal huts with twigs, grass, cow dung, and urine. Once this mixture dries, it's as strong as cement.

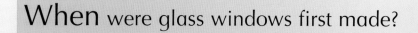

1756	1869	1885	1923	1932
Modern concrete invented	First canal opened to ships	First 10-story skyscraper built	Bulldozer first manufactured	First highway opened

When were glass windows first made?

People first invented glass in around 3000 BC, by heating sand, lime, and soda ash together in a furnace. For centuries, molten glass was shaped, then hardened by cooling to make small objects such as bottles. Sheet glass was first made for windows in the 13th century, but the panes were small and hard to see through. By the 19th century, factories were making clear sheets of rolled and polished plate glass.

ABOVE Today, glass is made by floating molten glass on a bed of molten tin—a process invented by the Englishman, Alastair Pilkington.

BELOW Steel frames are quick to put up to create the skeleton of a large building.

How is steel used in buildings?

Steel is used to make the frameworks of many buildings today, as well as all the bolts, bars, sheets, nails, rods, and pipes that hold buildings together. Molten steel can be molded into any shape, making this strong metal an ideal building material.

33

BUILDING KEY DATES

4000 BC	3500 BC	2000 BC	700 BC	AD 100
First canals in use	First oven-baked clay bricks	Clapper bridges used to cross rivers	First aqueduct built to carry water	Lifting machines first used for building

BUILDING MACHINES

What were the first building tools?

The ancient Egyptian pyramids are probably the most famous buildings in history. They were made possible by some simple, but important, inventions. In 3000 BC, Egyptian builders invented the plumb line, a weight on the end of a piece of string. They knew that their walls were perfectly upright when they matched the vertical line of the string. Around 2600 BC, Egyptian architects came up with a triangle to measure and build perfect right-angled corners on their buildings.

DID YOU KNOW?
Giant tunnel-boring machines were used to cut the Channel Tunnel under the English Channel between England and France. Completed in 1994, this train tunnel is over 32 miles long.

ABOVE LEFT A plumb line with a limestone plumb bob, or weight

LEFT A triangle made of bronze

When were cranes invented?

The Romans first used lifting machines powered by workers pulling on ropes in around AD 100. Modern cranes have a tall tower with a horizontal boom across the top. The long arm of the boom lifts and lowers materials using a system of cables attached to sets of pulleys. The short arm has a counterweight to balance the load and stop the crane from toppling over.

boom arm carrying lifting cables and hook

counterweight of concrete blocks

LEFT Huge tower cranes, like this one, are often fixed to the ground when working on construction sites.

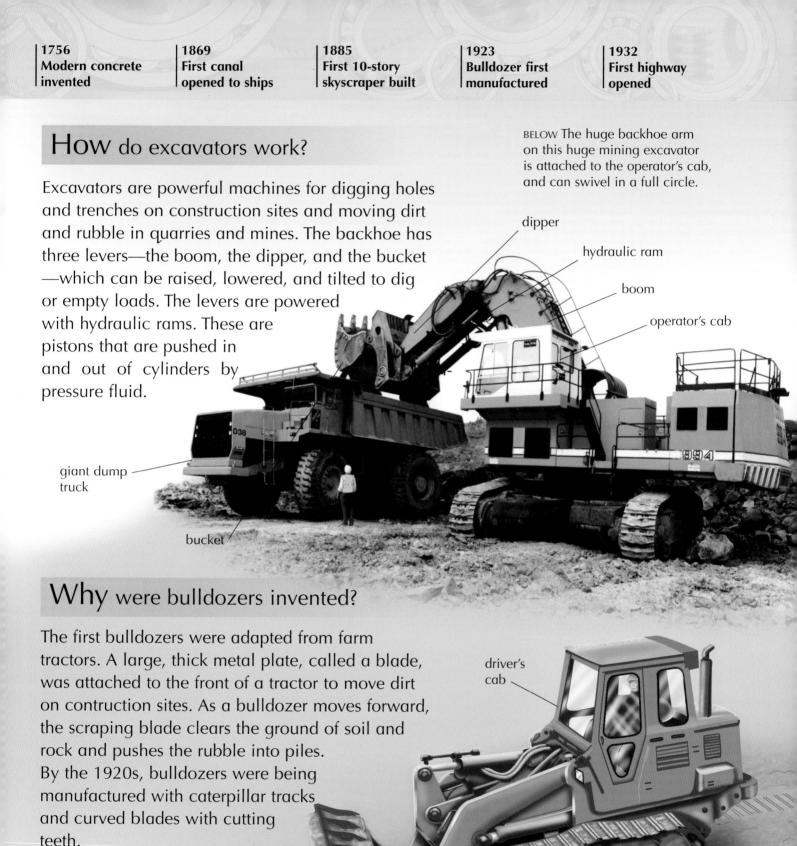

How do excavators work?

Excavators are powerful machines for digging holes and trenches on construction sites and moving dirt and rubble in quarries and mines. The backhoe has three levers—the boom, the dipper, and the bucket —which can be raised, lowered, and tilted to dig or empty loads. The levers are powered with hydraulic rams. These are pistons that are pushed in and out of cylinders by pressure fluid.

BELOW The huge backhoe arm on this huge mining excavator is attached to the operator's cab, and can swivel in a full circle.

dipper

hydraulic ram

boom

operator's cab

giant dump truck

bucket

Why were bulldozers invented?

The first bulldozers were adapted from farm tractors. A large, thick metal plate, called a blade, was attached to the front of a tractor to move dirt on contruction sites. As a bulldozer moves forward, the scraping blade clears the ground of soil and rock and pushes the rubble into piles. By the 1920s, bulldozers were being manufactured with caterpillar tracks and curved blades with cutting teeth.

driver's cab

blade

Caterpillar tracks enable a bulldozer to move over rough ground.

35

BUILDING KEY DATES

| 4000 BC First canals in use | 3500 BC First oven-baked clay bricks | 2000 BC Clapper bridges used to cross rivers | 700 BC First aqueduct built to carry water | AD 100 Lifting machines first used for building |

SKYSCRAPERS

When were skyscrapers invented?

In 1885, a 10-story-high office building in Chicago became the first of many skyscrapers. The American architect William le Baron Jenney first got the idea on a trip to Southeast Asia. Here, he saw houses made of reed matting strung on a framework of tree trunks. Jenney built the first high-rise building with a metal frame to support the floors and walls. This type of tall building quickly became known as a skyscraper.

ABOVE Chicago's Home Insurance Building designed by Jenney.

LEFT The famous Empire State Building in New York City was the world's tallest building when it was first built in 1931.

The skyscraper's weight is supported by lots of vertical steel columns anchored in the ground.

How are skyscrapers built?

In a brick or stone building, the walls of the ground floor have to hold up the weight of the rest of the structure. This means that even very thick walls can only support a building up to five stories high. Skyscrapers have an incredibly strong steel framework, rather like a skeleton, to carry the weight of the building. Lightweight walls slot into or hang from this framework.

Each floor is formed from steel girders that run horizontally between the columns.

DID YOU KNOW?
Most modern skyscrapers are built with self-cleaning glass, so there is no need for window cleaners. The glass has a special coating that stops dirt from sticking to it.

What is the world's tallest building?

The Taipei 101 in Taiwan is the world's tallest building. Completed in 2004, this skyscraper is nearly a quarter mile high and boasts a record 101 floors. The skyscraper is specially strengthened to withstand earthquakes, typhoons, and high winds.

RIGHT The Taipei 101 has the world's fastest elevators, which travel upward at a speed of 3,307 feet a minute. They whisk passengers to the top of the building in just 30 seconds!

The outer layer of glass and concrete is often called the curtain wall because of the way it hangs from the framework.

Who invented electric elevators?

The first powered elevator, or lift, was built in 1857 by the American, Elisha Graves Otis, for a New York department store. By 1903, the Otis company had perfected an electric elevator that made high-rise buildings a practical possibility. When passengers got in the elevator, a pulley system moved it up and down a shaft inside the building. Steel cables from the lift looped around a wheel, driven by an electric motor.

motorized wheel

steel cables

lift

counterweight

LEFT The elevator cables are joined to a heavy counterweight, which balances the load.

37

BUILDING KEY DATES

| 4000 BC
First canals
in use | 3500 BC
First oven-baked
clay bricks | 2000 BC
Clapper bridges
used to cross rivers | 700 BC
First aqueduct built
to carry water | AD 100
Lifting machines first
used for building |

ROADS

BELOW Roman roads were made up of several layers.

flag stones

drainage ditch

pebbles and gravel

stones in cement

sand

When were roads first built?

Many ancient civilizations, such as the Chinese and the Mayans, built stone-paved paths and roads. However, it was the Romans who were the first major road builders. From about 400 BC, they built a network of straight, wide, paved roads for their armies to move around their large empire. Better road surfaces were needed by the end of the 19th century, with the arrival of the automobile. Edgar Purnell Hooley invented tarmac in England in 1902. His mixture of coal tar and crushed stones formed a smooth road surface for the first time.

How are roads built today?

Many powerful road-building machines are needed to build major roads today. First, diggers and bulldozers clear the site of rocks and dirt. Scrapers level the ground and dump trucks remove the rubble. Graders smooth a layer of crushed stone before paving machines pour on a layer of hot asphalt—a black concretelike substance made from petroleum residue. Finally, heavy steam rollers run over the asphalt, as it cools and sets hard, to create a smooth road surface.

LEFT Steam rollers compress the asphalt with heavy iron rollers.

38

DID YOU KNOW?

Nighttime road markings called cat's eyes were invented in 1934 by the Englishman Percy Shaw. He got the idea from the shining eyes of a cat, which reflected in his headlights and saved him from driving off the road in the fog.

Where was the first highway built?

The first highway was opened in Germany in 1932, where it was known as an "autobahn". Today, large motorway networks link major towns and cities in many countries. Highways are wide roads and usually carry traffic on three lanes in each direction. Increasing numbers of cars, trucks, and coaches use these nonstop, fast-moving routes to travel long distances.

LEFT Spaghetti junctions are designed to keep traffic flowing, so there are no crossroads, traffic lights, or traffic circles.

What are spaghetti junctions?

Spaghetti junction is the nickname given to a tangle of major roads that meet in a complex system of loops, ramps and flyovers. The various freeways and highways are raised many feet above the ground on concrete pillars.

BUILDING KEY DATES

4000 BC	3500 BC	2000 BC	700 BC	AD 100
First canals in use	First oven-baked clay bricks	Clapper bridges used to cross rivers	First aqueduct built to carry water	Lifting machines first used for building

BRIDGES

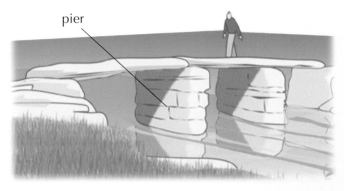

pier

ABOVE A stone clapper bridge

When were the first bridges built?

The earliest water crossings were logs laid over streams, but these simple beam bridges could not span wide rivers. People first built stone clapper bridges around 2000 BC. Slabs of stone were piled up in a river to make piers. The piers supported larger, flat stones that spanned the gaps and formed a pathway over the water.

Who invented arched bridges?

The Romans first used stone arches in their buildings and monuments. They soon realized that arches make strong structures and could be used to support bridges, too. Today's arched bridges are often made of steel or concrete and can span very wide gaps.

BELOW This arched bridge supports a railway line that runs straight over a river valley.

What is a suspension bridge?

Thousands of years ago, people in South America and Asia built simple rope bridges to help them cross rivers or canyons. Modern suspension bridges work in a similar way. The deck, or roadway, of a suspension bridge hangs from two main steel cables attached to tall support towers on both sides of the river. Wire hanger cables link the main cables to the deck.

BELOW A suspension bridge, like the Brooklyn Bridge in New York City is the best kind of bridge for spanning a wide crossing.

tower

main cable

People, trains, and traffic move across the deck.

BELOW The world's longest cantilever bridge is the Quebec Railway Bridge in Canada.

Built in 1917, the steel bridge spans 6,529 feet.

How are cantilever bridges built?

Cantilever bridges were invented to span wider rivers than beam and arched bridges could. They have a rigid metal framework that is divided into sections made up of strong, straight steel tubes arranged in triangular shapes. Each section is supported in the middle by a pier in the river so that the weight of the bridge is balanced out.

DID YOU KNOW?
The Akashi Kaikyo Bridge in Japan is the world's longest suspension bridge. It has a main span of 6,529 feet.

Each half of the bridge balances on a supporting pier.

41

BUILDING KEY DATES

| 4000 BC
First canals
in use | 3500 BC
First oven-baked
clay bricks | 2000 BC
Clapper bridges
used to cross rivers | 700 BC
First aqueduct built
to carry water | AD 100
Lifting machines first
used for building |

CANALS

Why were canals invented?

Canals are waterways or artificial rivers that people build to move heavy goods over long distances. The oldest-known canals were built in Mesopotamia in around 4000 BC. From the mid-18th century, long canal boats called barges, or narrowboats, were transporting large loads of coal and other heavy goods on the canal networks.

BELOW Today, goods barges still operate on major canal networks.

BELOW The Pont du Gard aqueduct in France was built by the Romans in around 19 BC. The water channel ran along the top.

The first level was a road bridge.

What are aqueducts?

The earliest aqueducts were channels in the ground built to carry water to ancient cities. Some were large enough for ships to travel along. Aqueducts were also built above ground so that canals or waterways could bridge the gap over valleys. The first large aqueduct was built by the Assyrians in around 700 BC. It was 33 feet high and 985 feet long and carried water to the capital city of Nineveh in the Middle East.

How do canal locks work?

Locks help canal boats travel up or downhill. They are used to lift or lower boats when the water level changes. A lock is a section of canal big enough to take at least one barge. It is sealed with two watertight gates at each end. By opening paddles, or valves, in one set of gates, water either runs into the lock to raise the boat to a higher level, or runs out of the lock to lower the boat down.

Sealed lock gates hold back the upper water level.

Paddles in the lower lock gates open to let the water out and drop the barge down.

DID YOU KNOW?
Horses pulled early barges up and down canals. Towpaths were built beside the canals for the horses to walk along.

BELOW Cargo ships use the Suez Canal in Egypt and the Panama canal in Central America as shortcuts between continents.

When was the first ship canal built?

Ship canals are giant canals that connect seas and oceans. Ship canals make it quicker for cargo ships to travel around the world. The Suez Canal in Egypt, which joins the Red Sea and the Mediterranean Sea, was the first canal to be opened to ships in 1869. Around 25,000 ships a year use this canal to travel between Europe and Southeast Asia, rather than sail the long way around the tip of Africa.

ENERGY

Waterwheels, wooden windmills, electricity, and nuclear power plants help us provide the power that makes machines work for us. Find out what makes steam engines work, how scientists find oil and gas hidden deep under the ground, and how hydroelectric power plants use moving water to make electricity. Discover how renewable energy, such as tidal and geothermal power, can light and heat our homes, and find out about the cars that run on sunlight instead of gasoline.

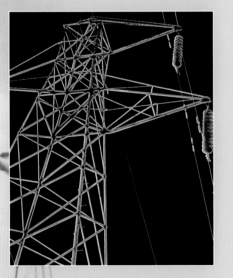
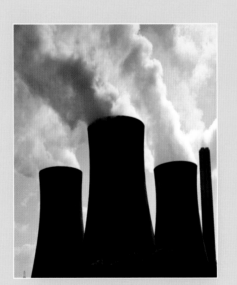

ENERGY KEY DATES

600 BC	30 BC	AD 1712	1800	1831
Windmill invented to grind flour	Waterwheels used to power water mills	First steam engine invented	Battery first used to produce electricity	Electrical generator invented

WIND AND WATER POWER

When was the waterwheel invented?

In around 100 BC, the ancient Greeks invented the first waterwheels. These turned horizontally in fast-moving stream water and drove grinding stones to make flour. By 30 BC, the Romans were building large upright waterwheels to power water mills. Water mills continued to be built in this way for many centuries.

Windmill sails are turned to face into the wind.

How do windmills work?

The windmill was invented in Persia, now called Iran, in 600 BC. It enabled people to mill flour in places where there was no running water. The earliest windmills turned vertically on a central wooden spindle with cloth sails at the top and millstones at the bottom. In the 12th century, European windmills were designed with a horizontal spindle, called a wind shaft, attached to four large wooden sails.

The wind drives around the sails, which spin the wind shaft.

The wind shaft powers a system of cogs and vertical drive shafts.

The vertical drive shafts turn the millstones to grind flour.

DID YOU KNOW?
The Three Gorges Dam in China is the biggest hydroelectric power project in the world. Once it is built, the dam will have 26 electricity generators and a reservoir 372 miles long!

What is hydroelectric power?

A hydroelectric power plant converts the natural energy of running water into electricity. In most plants, a dam is built across a river and collects water in a reservoir. As some of this water flows down through pipes, it travels with increasing speed and force. Inside the plant, the rushing water turns a wheeled motor, called a turbine, which drives an electricity generator. Power lines then carry the electricity to people's homes and businesses.

RIGHT Water from the power plant flows back into the river further downstream.

dam

Inside a hydroelectric dam

generator

power lines

turbine

raised river level

reservoir

Dam gates are opened to let the river run through when the water level is high.

Where was the first hydroelectric dam built?

The world's first hydroelectric power plant was built on a river in Wisconsin in 1882. The dam produced enough electricity to power the machinery in two paper mills, as well as the lighting in the mill owner's home nearby.

ENERGY KEY DATES

600 BC	30 BC	AD 1712	1800	1831
Windmill invented to grind flour	Waterwheels used to power water mills	First steam engine invented	Battery first used to produce electricity	Electrical generator invented

FOSSIL FUELS

What are fossil fuels?

Fossil fuels are formed from the remains of dead prehistoric plants and animals that became buried under thick mud. These remains were squashed together under layers of rock and slowly, over millions of years, turned into coal, gas, or oil. Fossil fuels are removed from the ground through mining or drilling. When burned, these fuels produce heat, light, and power for machines or for generating electricity. They also release polluting gases into the air.

LEFT Coal is burned in furnaces to heat water and make steam, which is used to power machines.

How do scientists find oil and gas?

Around 1910, scientists began using the seismograph to locate the gaps in rocks deep underground or beneath the seabed, where oil or gas may be found. Dynamite or air gun explosions are used to create sound waves. These reflect off underground rock layers and are recorded by the seismograph.

The seismograph is located on board the survey boat.

air gun explosion

Hydrophones in the water detect the sound waves, which are recorded by the seismograph.

The rock layers reflect the sound waves.

ABOVE The modern seismograph was invented in 1880. It also detects tiny underground movements to help predict earthquakes.

BELOW Early gas street lights were lit by hand.

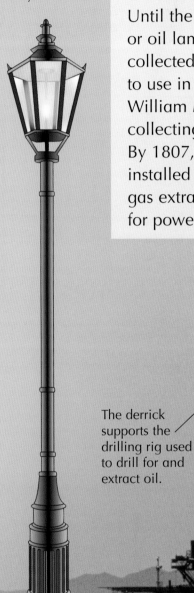

When was gas lighting invented?

Until the 1700s, people mostly used candles or oil lamps for lighting. A few people collected natural gas from underground to use in lamps. In 1792, English engineer William Murdoch invented a way of collecting gas produced by heating coal. By 1807, the first coal gas street lights were installed in London, UK. Today, most natural gas extracted from the ground is used as fuel for power plants.

DID YOU KNOW?

The Petronius platform in the Gulf of Mexico is one of the world's tallest structures. This giant, deep-sea oil and gas rig stands 2,000 feet high. It is anchored 1,750 feet above the ocean floor.

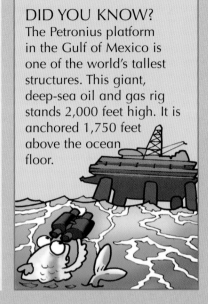

Where was the first oil rig built?

As far back as AD 350, the Chinese were drilling oil wells, using drill bits attached to hollow bamboo poles. The first modern oil well was drilled in Asia in 1848. Then in 1947, the first offshore drilling platform was built to obtain oil and gas from below the seabed in the Gulf of Mexico. Today, many offshore oil rigs are anchored in ocean water over one mile deep.

The derrick supports the drilling rig used to drill for and extract oil.

LEFT The oil platform has living accommodation where oil workers rest and sleep when they are off duty.

A steel framework supports the platform underneath the sea.

ENERGY KEY DATES

600 BC	30 BC	AD 1712	1800	1831
Windmill invented to grind flour	Waterwheels used to power water mills	First steam engine invented	Battery first used to produce electricity	Electrical generator invented

STEAM POWER

BELOW Watt's steam engine

When was the steam engine invented?

In 1712, a steam-powered piston engine was developed for the first time by the Englishman Thomas Newcomen. His engine burned coal to make steam. The steam powered pumps, which removed floodwater from mines.

How did steam engines work?

In 1769, the Scottish engineer James Watt improved Newcomen's steam engine. In Watt's engine, the steam was forced into a cylinder pushing the piston up. The steam was then condensed by a jet of cold water. This created a vacuum, which let the piston fall back down the cylinder. The up-and-down movement of the piston could power pumps or drive a rocking beam, which turned the wheels of all kinds of factory machines.

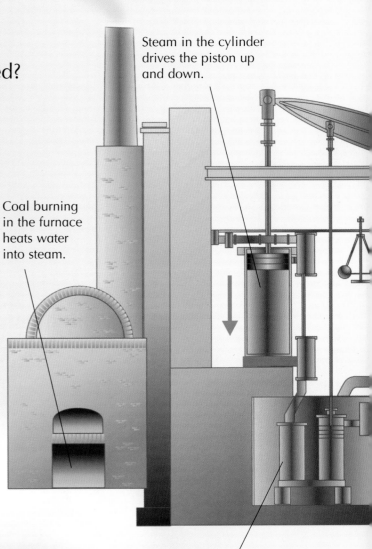

Steam in the cylinder drives the piston up and down.

Coal burning in the furnace heats water into steam.

condenser

LEFT Steam engines were later modified to power railroad locomotives and steamships.

75029

The rocking beam drives the wheel round

BELOW Parsons' *Turbinia* steamship

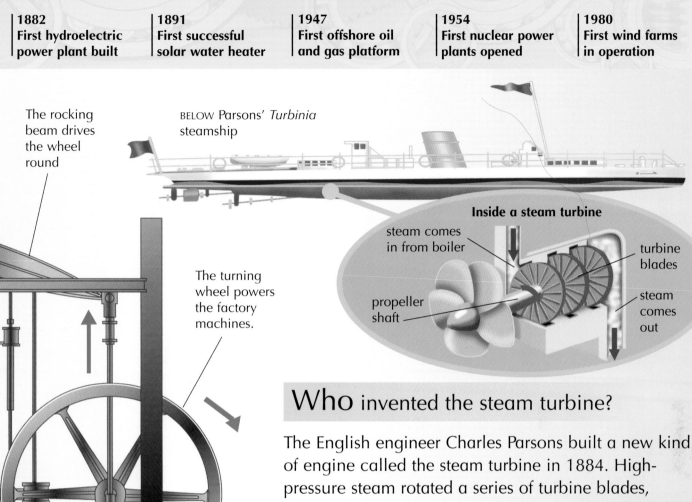

Inside a steam turbine

steam comes in from boiler

turbine blades

propeller shaft

steam comes out

The turning wheel powers the factory machines.

Who invented the steam turbine?

The English engineer Charles Parsons built a new kind of engine called the steam turbine in 1884. High-pressure steam rotated a series of turbine blades, which generated the power to drive machines. In 1897, Parsons launched his steamship, the *Turbinia,* to test his invention. The ship raced through the water powered by three turbine engines turning nine propellers.

What fuels today's steam-powered cars?

In 2004, British engineers produced *Inspiration*, a fast, futuristic car propelled by a jet of steam. Steam-driven engines can use any fuel, including solar energy. This means they make less polluting exhaust fumes. In the future, designers hope that steam-powered cars might be an environmentally friendly alternative to vehicles with gasoline engines.

DID YOU KNOW?
In 1906, a steam-powered car, called the *Stanley Rocket*, set the world land-speed record at 128 miles per hour. The record still stands for steam-powered cars today.

RIGHT *Inspiration* has a steam engine that runs on propane gas.

ENERGY KEY DATES

600 BC	30 BC	AD 1712	1800	1831
Windmill invented to grind flour	Waterwheels used to power water mills	First steam engine invented	Battery first used to produce electricity	Electrical generator invented

ELECTRICITY

Who invented the battery?

In 1780, the Italian scientist Alessandro Volta realized that a chemical reaction between a dead frog, a metal knife, and a metal table created an electric charge that made the dead frog jolt! Later, in 1800, Volta made the first battery from a pile of zinc and copper disks separated by cloth soaked in saltwater. When connected, a chemical reaction between the metals and the saltwater produced an electric current.

RIGHT Volta's pile battery

pairs of zinc and copper disks

DID YOU KNOW?
Batteries may soon be replaced by nonpolluting fuel cells. These convert the gases hydrogen and oxygen into water to produce electricity.

BELOW Faraday also built the first electromagnetic generator, using a fixed magnet, in 1832.

A copper disk rotates between the poles of a magnet.

A small electric current flows through the wire.

magnet

What is an electrical generator?

In 1831, the English scientist Michael Faraday demonstrated the first simple electrical generator. When a magnet was moved through a loop of copper wire, the magnetism generated an electric current, which flowed through the wire. It was another 50 years before the first large generator providing electric power was built. This used a spinning magnet inside a giant coil of metal wire to create an electric current.

A voltmeter measures the strength of the electric current.

When was the electric lightbulb invented?

It was only when the lightbulb was invented, in 1879, that it became possible to light buildings with electricity. A lightbulb is a glass globe with a wire inside, called a filament. The filament glows when electricity passes through it and produces light. Electric lamps first became reliable when the American inventor Thomas Edison discovered the carbon filament. This produced light for a long time before it burned out.

filament

How do we get our electricity?

A coal-fired powered plant burns coal in a furnace to boil water into steam. The high-pressure steam drives turbines linked to large electrical generators. These convert the spinning movement of the turbines into electrical energy, which is carried along power lines to homes, factories, and businesses.

RIGHT Electricity either flows along cables buried in the ground or is carried by tall towers called pylons.

cooling towers

turbine and generator house

coal store

ENERGY KEY DATES

| 600 BC Windmill invented to grind flour | 30 BC Waterwheels used to power water mills | AD 1712 First steam engine invented | 1800 Battery first used to produce electricity | 1831 Electrical generator invented |

NUCLEAR POWER

Who first split the atom?

In 1938, the German scientists Otto Hahn and Fritz Strassmann first discovered they could split the atom of a rare metal called uranium-235. Atoms are tiny particles of matter that can only be seen under a powerful microscope. When the uranium atoms started to split, or fission, they released huge amounts of heat energy. As the atom fragments hit other atoms, they also split and created more heat in a chain reaction —producing nuclear energy for the first time.

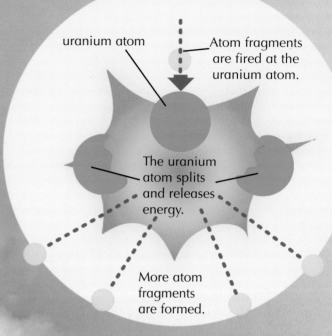

uranium atom

Atom fragments are fired at the uranium atom.

The uranium atom splits and releases energy.

More atom fragments are formed.

ABOVE Atoms can be split to create nuclear energy.

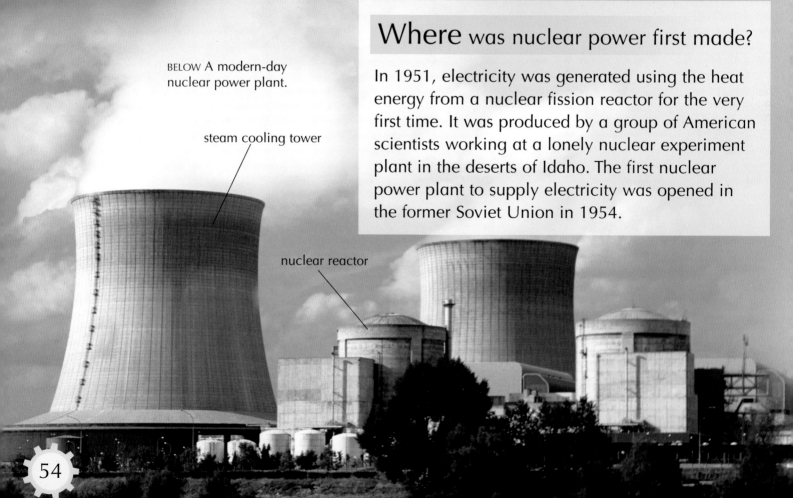

BELOW A modern-day nuclear power plant.

steam cooling tower

nuclear reactor

Where was nuclear power first made?

In 1951, electricity was generated using the heat energy from a nuclear fission reactor for the very first time. It was produced by a group of American scientists working at a lonely nuclear experiment plant in the deserts of Idaho. The first nuclear power plant to supply electricity was opened in the former Soviet Union in 1954.

How do nuclear fuel rods work?

Nuclear power plants run on uranium fuel. Pellets of uranium are stacked inside metal fuel rods. The fuel rods are gathered together in bundles and placed in a reactor full of water, surrounded by control rods. When the control rods are raised out of the reactor, the uranium atoms start to split and the water temperature begins to rise. The boiling water is used to make steam, which drives turbines linked to electrical generators.

Control rods are raised or lowered to control the nuclear reaction.

The fuel rods are grouped into bundles and placed under water in the reactor.

uranium pellets inside a fuel rod

DID YOU KNOW?
Nuclear-powered naval submarines can cruise nonstop for 25 years without needing to refuel.

What makes nuclear power safe?

Uranium gives off harmful radiation as well as heat during nuclear fission. So nuclear power reactors are built out of several layers of very thick metal and concrete. This prevents radioactive material from escaping into the environment. Used nuclear fuel rods are also highly radioactive. They are cooled down in water for many years, before being loaded into special containers and carefully transported by road or rail to a disposal site. Here, the radioactive waste is buried in tunnels deep underground, far away from people.

dry, stable rock

shaft

The fuel rods are buried in tunnels.

Nuclear waste remains radioactive underground for about 1,000 years.

LEFT Isolated disposal sites were invented as a means of dealing with high-level radioactive waste.

55

ENERGY KEY DATES

| 600 BC
Windmill invented
to grind flour | 30 BC
Waterwheels used to
power water mills | AD 1712
First steam engine
invented | 1800
Battery first used to
produce electricity | 1831
Electrical generator
invented |

SOLAR POWER

What is solar power?

Solar power is energy that comes from sunlight. The Sun gives out an incredible amount of heat and light energy. As early as 400 BC, people used magnifying glasses to focus the Sun's rays on fuel to light fires. By 4 BC, the Romans were building bathhouses with large, south-facing windows to catch the Sun's warmth. Today, solar power is collected and used to heat water and buildings, and also to generate electricity.

BELOW A solar oven has a reflective lid to bounce sunlight onto the cooking pots inside.

Who invented the solar oven?

In 1767 the Swiss scientist Horace de Saussure built the first solar oven. He designed a glass-covered, insulated box, which trapped heat from the light of the Sun. Although it needed a sunny day to work, Saussure's oven was perfectly able to cook food. Simple solar ovens are still used around the world today. They cook at high temperatures and are free to use because they need no fuel.

LEFT Solar power plants can operate in sunny regions. They use hundreds of solar panels to heat oil in pipes. The hot oil is used to create steam. This drives steam turbines that generate electricity.

sunlight

Solar panels have dark-colored plates because dark colors absorb heat well.

hot-water pipe

How do solar water heaters work?

The American inventor Clarence Kemp produced the world's first successful solar water heater in 1891. Today, a similar design is used in solar roof panels, which are used to heat water in many homes. Sunlight passes through the glass on top of the panel and the heat is collected by an absorber plate below. Cold water flows through pipes in the middle of the solar panel and, once heated, is stored in a hot-water tank inside the building.

cold-water pipe

The hot-water tank stores water for future use in sinks, bathtubs, and showers.

DID YOU KNOW?
In space, there is an unlimited supply of sunlight and so all satellites are powered by solar cells. Each satellite carries panels with as many as 40,000 photovoltaic cells.

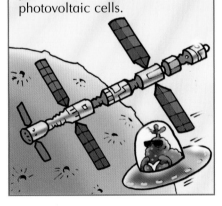

Where were solar cells first used?

The French scientist Alexandre-Edmond Becquerel first invented a solar cell to produce electricity from sunlight in 1839. However, these early solar, or photovoltaic, cells were not very efficient. In 1954, a group of American scientists realized that photovoltaic cells containing silicon could capture light from the Sun and convert it directly into electricity. By assembling many cells together in solar panels, it was possible to generate a large amount of electricity.

BELOW This car runs on solar energy. It carries panels of photovoltaic cells, which make electricity to power the motor.

solar panels

ENERGY KEY DATES

600 BC	30 BC	AD 1712	1800	1831
Windmill invented to grind flour	Waterwheels used to power water mills	First steam engine invented	Battery first used to produce electricity	Electrical generator invented

NATURAL ENERGY SOURCES

A small electrical generator is positioned behind the blades.

turbine blades

When were wind turbines invented?

Wind turbines were first used in the 1940s to turn the natural energy of the wind into electricity. They powered remote farms in the US. Today's wind turbines have two or three propeller-like blades, which are mounted on tall towers up to 100 feet high. As the wind blows, the turbine blades rotate and drive a small generator that produces electricity. Since the early 1980s, groups of wind turbines, called wind farms, have been built both on land and out at sea.

How is natural waste used as fuel?

Waste materials from plants, such as wood chips, sawdust from sawmills, or straw from farms, are called biomass fuels. Biogas can also be made from animal waste, such as manure. These fuels can be burned to heat water and make steam for power plants.

BELOW A digester produces biogas from animal manure. The manure is stored in a tank for a few weeks, where it rots and gives off gas.

Biogas is collected from the top of the digester.

Inside a wind turbine

driveshaft

gears

electricity generator

A drive turns the blades to face into the wind.

turbine blade

Leftover manure is piped out of the tank.

58

1882
First hydroelectric
power plant built

1891
First successful
solar water heater

1947
First offshore oil
and gas platform

1954
First nuclear power
plants opened

1980
First wind farms
in operation

Where was the first tidal power plant?

The movement of the sea carries energy in the form of tides, currents, and waves. A tidal power plant uses this natural energy to produce electricity. The world's first and largest-ever tidal power plant was opened in 1966 on the Rance River in France. A huge dam, called a barrage, was built across the river estuary where it meets the sea. As the tides come in and go out, the water flows through tunnels in the barrage, turning turbines that drive electricity generators.

LEFT The Rance River tidal barrage in France

DID YOU KNOW?
Scientists have invented a way to turn pig manure into biomass diesel to power cars. One pig can produce around 21 gallons of diesel in a lifetime.

What is geothermal energy?

The temperatures in the center of the Earth are hot enough to melt rock. In some places, this molten rock is not far below ground and generates natural heat, called geothermal energy. Wells are drilled into the ground and cold water is pumped down to the hot rocks. The water heats up and turns into steam. This is piped back above ground and used to turn turbines that drive electricity generators.

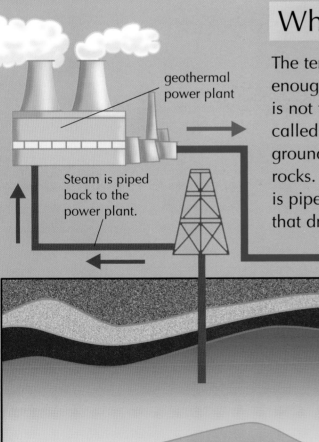

geothermal power plant

Steam is piped back to the power plant.

Cold water is pumped down to the hot rocks.

hot, molten rock

MANUFACTURING

Incredible inventions, such as spinning wheels and industrial robots, have helped us speed up the way we make things. Find out how jets of air or water help to make the fabric used for the clothes we wear, and how your old soft-drink cans are turned into new ones overnight. Learn about how soap is made and why factories use conveyor belts. Discover why so many of the things around us are made of plastic and how robots, instead of people, are making new cars.

MANUFACTURING KEY DATES

| 5000 BC
Loom invented
for weaving cloth | AD 1000
Spinning wheels
used to make yarn | 1733
Flying shuttle first
used for weaving | 1764
Spinning jenny
invented | 1771
First factory with
powered machines |

SPINNING AND WEAVING

DID YOU KNOW?
The American Eli Whitney had the idea for a cotton-cleaning machine in 1793, after seeing a cat use its claws. His invention, called a gin, had rows of sharp hooks that separated cotton fibers from their sticky seeds.

thread winds onto
the spindles

RIGHT Hargreaves'
spinning jenny

Who invented the spinning wheel?

Spinning wheels are machines that help to make strong thread or yarn. They were invented by textile workers making cloth in Asia, in around AD 1000. The operator spins a large wheel on a frame. This pulls and twists together short fibers of cotton or wool into long continuous yarn, which is wound onto a spindle. In 1764, the Englishman James Hargreaves invented the spinning jenny machine that could wind thread onto many spindles at a time.

spinning wheel
handle

cotton fibers

When was the loom invented?

The handloom was invented in around 5000 BC for weaving fabrics or carpets from yarn. One set of yarn, called the warp, is tied vertically to the wooden loom. Then another set of yarn, called the weft, is woven in and out across the warp to make cloth. In 1733, the Englishman John Kay invented the flying shuttle. This was a spindle with weft yarns wrapped around it that could be quickly knocked back and forth across the loom. It made weaving much quicker.

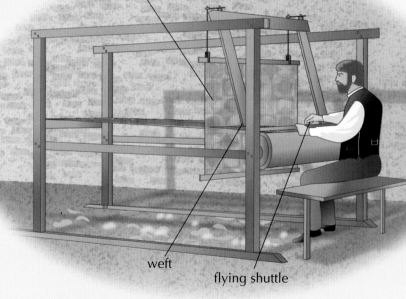

warp

weft

flying shuttle

ABOVE Kay's flying shuttle loom

What did the first factory produce?

In the earliest factories, textile workers made cloth completely by hand. The world's first factory with powered machinery was built by the Englishman Richard Arkwright in 1771. His cotton mill in Cromford, England, employed lots of workers. They operated spinning machines, invented by Arkwright, and looms to weave cotton cloth. The machines were first powered by waterwheels and later by steam engines. Arkwright built houses nearby for his mill workers to live in.

BELOW Cromford mill was built beside a river and used the water to power its spinning and weaving machines.

How do industrial looms work?

The industrial looms of today are huge, computerized machines and are housed in vast factory warehouses. They operate without flying shuttles. Now, jets of high-pressure air or water are used to shoot weft yarns at high speed between the warp. Each loom is programmed to select different yarn colors and create complex patterns in the cloth it weaves. One textile worker can look after 20 looms at the same time.

LEFT Traditional industrial looms are still used in small factories today.

BELOW Colorful spools of yarn used for weaving.

63

MANUFACTURING KEY DATES

5000 BC	AD 1000	1733	1764	1771
Loom invented for weaving cloth	Spinning wheels used to make yarn	Flying shuttle first used for weaving	Spinning jenny invented	First factory with powered machines

FACTORY PRODUCTS

BELOW Baekeland named his discovery Bakelite. This hard plastic was used to make many everyday objects, like this telephone.

When was plastic invented?

In the late 1800s, natural materials such as bone, shell, and ivory were used to make buttons, knife handles and other products. These were expensive, so inventors created a new material, called celluloid, in 1863. This artificial material was produced by adding chemicals to cotton fibers and was the first type of plastic. In 1909, a chemist from New York, invented the first true plastic made just from chemicals. Leo Baekeland discovered that his sticky mixture could be molded into shapes and baked hard.

LEFT Celluloid was used to make objects that looked like ivory or bone, such as this baby's hairbrush.

What is plastic used for today?

Plastic has quickly become the major industrial material because it is waterproof, easily molded into shapes, and cheap to produce. Different plastics can be soft or hard, flexible or stiff, colored or transparent, depending on the chemical ingredients used to make them. Factory-made plastic objects are all around us, from the insides of cars and fridges to toys, clothing, CDs, and cell phones.

BELOW In the past, outdoor toys, like this tricycle, were made of heavy, sharp metal that rusted easily. Today's trikes are built out of colorful plastic.

RIGHT Many liquid products, such as laundry detergent, are packaged in plastic bottles. These have replaced heavy, glass bottles that could smash if dropped.

Why is aluminum recycled in factories?

Since 1958, aluminum has been used to make cans for drinks. Aluminum is a light metal that can be extracted from rocks and clays. But many new cans are actually made from old ones. At a recycling plant, waste cans are melted down and poured into molds to form metal ingots. The ingots are taken to a factory where huge rollers press them into thin sheets of aluminum. Machines cut the sheets into pieces and join them together to produce new cans ready for filling.

DID YOU KNOW?
People throw away millions of plastic bottles each day, but they are put to good use if recycled. They are shredded and turned into polyester fibers to make new carpets, clothing, or more bottles.

How is soap made?

Bars of soap are made by heating plant oils or animal fats together with an alkali, such as wood ash. This produces soap and a substance called glycerine. In a factory, the glycerine is removed, and the soap is dried before perfumes and colorings are added. The soap is then cut into pieces, pressed into shape, and wrapped into the bars we buy in the stores.

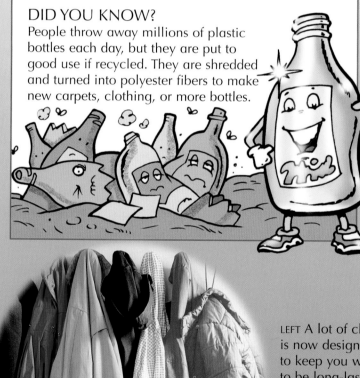

LEFT A lot of clothing is now designed to keep you warm, to be long-lasting, waterproof, or fast-drying, thanks to new fabrics made with plastic fibers.

MANUFACTURING KEY DATES

| 5000 BC Loom invented for weaving cloth | AD 1000 Spinning wheels used to make yarn | 1733 Flying shuttle first used for weaving | 1764 Spinning jenny invented | 1771 First factory with powered machines |

MASS PRODUCTION

BELOW Brunel's factory produced 130,000 pulley blocks a year.

Where did mass production begin?

In the first factories, one worker would often make a whole product from start to finish. Then in England in 1802, French-born engineer Marc Isambard Brunel began mass-producing wooden pulley blocks for ships' rigging. His factory used 45 different steam-driven machines. To speed up production, each worker had a single job to do to each pulley block before passing it on to the next worker.

Who created moving assembly lines?

Ransom E. Olds created the first moving assembly line in his American automobile factory in 1901. He started using conveyor belts to speed up his car production process. The conveyor belts carried the cars to workers in different parts of the factory. Workers quickly added the same part to every passing car. The faster production times meant that assembly-line cars could be sold more cheaply.

RIGHT Olds' assembly line was copied by other early car manufacturers, such as Henry Ford in the US.

When were industrial robots invented?

One problem with assembly lines is that workers can get bored repeating the same job, and tired machine operators can make mistakes. A solution was found in 1961, when an industrial robot was installed in an American car factory for the first time. Programmed by computer, the robot carried out the dangerous job of unloading and stacking hot metal parts from a machine.

DID YOU KNOW?
Sensors in computer-controlled robotic arms make sure that they repeat exactly the same movements again and again—without ever getting tired!

RIGHT Industrial robots are quick and accurate. They perform many manufacturing tasks, such as welding, painting, assembling parts, and testing finished products.

A robotic arm has moving joints powered by motors.

What is mass customization?

Mass customization is when goods are made to suit a customer's needs using mass production processes. Modern computer technology makes it possible for factories to build the basic components of a product, such as a car, and then put together a specially made version. For instance, customers might order a specific paint color for their car, a personalized computer, or a CD with their own selection of songs.

Early cars were put together quickly on a conveyor belt.

67

TRANSPORTATION

Since ancient times, people have found ingenious ways to transport themselves and their goods on land, over water, and in the air. Learn about simple dug-out canoes, ancient wheeled carts, the first bicycles. Find out about public transportation, such as horse-drawn buses and steam trains, and the development of faster, powered vehicles like trucks and cars. Discover when people first crossed oceans in sailing ships, and how inventions, such as hot-air balloons and helicopters, finally conquered the skies.

TRANSPORTATION KEY DATES

7000 BC	3500 BC	AD 400	1783	1825
First dugout canoes and rafts	First sailing boats and wheeled carts	Catamaran boat invented	First hot-air balloon flight	First steam railroad in use

BUSES AND TRUCKS

How did people first transport goods?

Between 7000 and 4000 BC, people first used sleds for hauling goods over land. Around 5000 BC, people started to train animals, such as donkeys and mules, to carry loads on their backs to pull them along on large wooden racks. Then around 4000 BC, the wheel was invented in Mesopotamia. This led to the development of wheeled carts that could be pulled by animals.

ABOVE Mesopotamian war chariot

DID YOU KNOW?
The longest freight trucks in the world drive on the straight, flat roads of the Australian outback. These monsters tow three or four giant trailers and are nicknamed "road trains".

When were coaches invented?

People began to use large, four-wheeled coaches drawn by horses in the 1600s. Coaches carried several people and luggage and had a roof to protect passengers from the weather. From the mid-1700s, long-distance coaches were called "stagecoaches" because the journey was made in stages. At each stop, passengers got off, and the four tired horses were replaced with fresh ones to maintain a speed of about 7 miles an hour.

LEFT Stagecoach services were the first kind of public transportation.

1870
High Wheeler
bicycle invented

1885
First gasoline-
powered automobile

1903
First successful
airplane flight

1939
Modern-style
helicopter invented

1976
First supersonic
passenger plane

ABOVE A horse-drawn omnibus

Where was the first bus service?

The first omnibus, or bus, pulled by horses ran in Paris, France, in 1828. It had a carriage big enough to carry several passengers, who sat on wooden benches. The omnibus was slowly replaced by trams, which ran along tracks through city streets. The first horse-drawn tram service started in 1832 in New York City. Since the 1880s, most trams have been powered by electricity and today's buses usually run on gas or diesel.

LEFT Double-decker buses operated in London, England.

Who invented refrigerated trucks?

The American Frederick Jones invented the first refrigerated truck in 1935 to keep produce fresh on long journeys. Today, most trucks have a fan to circulate air, a cooling unit to absorb heat, and a thermostat to maintain the right temperature. The refrigerated area is insulated to keep cold air in and warm air out.

RIGHT A refrigerated truck carries fresh food long distances.

71

TRANSPORTATION KEY DATES

| 7000 BC
First dugout canoes
and rafts | 3500 BC
First sailing boats
and wheeled carts | AD 400
Catamaran boat
invented | 1783
First hot-air
balloon flight | 1825
First steam
railroad in use |

BIKES

When was the first bicycle made?

DID YOU KNOW?
Before 1888, wooden wheels and iron tires gave cyclists a very bumpy ride. Bicycles today have rubber pneumatic, or air-filled, tires, thanks to Scottish inventor John Dunlop.

The very first bicycle, called the hobby horse, was invented in 1819. It was made of wood, had no pedals, and you pushed it along the ground with your feet. The first bike with pedals to power the back wheels was the *velocipede*, invented in 1839. However, the first bicycle that looked like those we ride today was the *Rover* safety bicycle. It was built in 1885 by the British engineer John Starley. It had a chain, a diamond-shaped frame, and equal-sized wheels with spokes.

RIGHT The *Rover* safety bicycle

What was the penny farthing?

British engineers invented the penny farthing (called a High Wheeler in the US) in 1870. This odd bicycle was named after two coins of the time—the large penny and the small farthing—because of the difference in the size of its wheels. Each turn of the pedals made the bicycle travel a long way on the large front wheel. Unfortunately, this high-wheeled bike was unsafe to ride and was often in accidents. So when the safety bike was invented in 1885, the penny farthing soon disappeared.

LEFT The penny farthing's front wheel measured up to 5 feet in diameter.

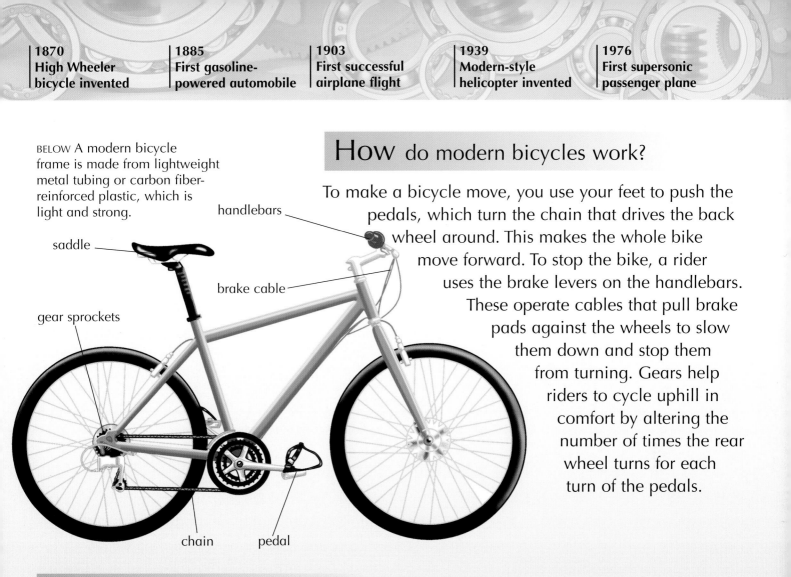

BELOW A modern bicycle frame is made from lightweight metal tubing or carbon fiber-reinforced plastic, which is light and strong.

saddle

handlebars

brake cable

gear sprockets

chain

pedal

How do modern bicycles work?

To make a bicycle move, you use your feet to push the pedals, which turn the chain that drives the back wheel around. This makes the whole bike move forward. To stop the bike, a rider uses the brake levers on the handlebars. These operate cables that pull brake pads against the wheels to slow them down and stop them from turning. Gears help riders to cycle uphill in comfort by altering the number of times the rear wheel turns for each turn of the pedals.

Who invented the motorcycle?

In 1885, German engineers Gottlieb Daimler and Wilhelm Maybach designed the first two-wheeled motorcycle to run on a gas engine. Today's motorcycles have a steel frame with the engine, gearbox, saddle, fuel tank, and other parts attached to it. The engine drives a shaft, or chain, that turns the back wheel. As with a bicycle, it is the back wheel that pushes the motorcycle forward.

RIGHT The police use motorcycles to patrol busy highways.

engine   fuel tank   chain   exhaust

TRANSPORTATION KEY DATES

| 7000 BC | 3500 BC | AD 400 | 1783 | 1825 |
| First dugout canoes and rafts | First sailing boats and wheeled carts | Catamaran boat invented | First hot-air balloon flight | First steam railroad in use |

AUTOS

RIGHT Karl Benz's first automobile only had three wheels.

internal combustion engine

When was the automobile invented?

German engineer Karl Benz invented the first gasoline-powered automobile in 1885. By using the earlier invention in1859 of the internal combustion engine, Benz was able to build a practical motorized vehicle. However, his car traveled very slowly and passengers sat up high and in the open. Early cars were expensive and it wasn't until 1910, when Henry Ford began making cheaper mass-produced cars in the US, that more people could afford to drive.

Why do car engines need gasoline?

ABOVE Drivers refuel their cars at a gas station. The gasoline is pumped through a hose with a nozzle into the fuel tank.

RIGHT There are usually four cylinders in a car engine. Inside each one the spark plug ignites a mixture of fuel and air, which explodes and pushes the piston down.

Modern cars have an internal combustion engine. The engine burns gasoline or diesel inside a cylinder to produce the energy to propel the car along. The burning fuel drives a piston up and down, which powers the driveshaft. This then turns the wheel axles to make the car move. A battery provides electricity for the starter motor and spark plugs, which together start the engine.

The driver uses pedals and other controls to speed up or brake the car and to change gear.

spark plug

fuel and air in

exhaust fumes out

Inside a car engine cylinder

piston

driveshaft

The gearbox changes the amount of power going to the car's wheels.

The driveshaft connects the gearbox to the rear axle.

How fast can race cars go?

On the straight stretch of a race track, specially built race cars can zoom along at 186 miles per hour. Race cars reach these high speeds because their engines are more powerful and work faster than those in normal vehicles. Race cars are also built low to the ground and specially shaped to reduce air resistance.

ABOVE The checkered flag marks the finish line.

DID YOU KNOW?
The world's cleanest cars are air-powered. Their piston engines run on compressed air, which is stored in tanks underneath the vehicle.

driver's cockpit

Wide rubber tires grip the road.

The front and rear wings on this Indy car help to keep the vehicle pressed to the road at high speeds.

fuel tank

The exhaust pipe releases waste gases from the engine.

What are battery-powered cars?

Battery-powered cars are electric vehicles that run on batteries. Their invention came about because of people's concerns about pollution caused by gas exhaust fumes. However, electric car batteries are big and heavy. They can only store enough power for a vehicle to travel a certain distance before they need to be plugged into an electricity supply and recharged.

TRANSPORTATION KEY DATES

7000 BC	3500 BC	AD 400	1783	1825
First dugout canoes and rafts	First sailing boats and wheeled carts	Catamaran boat invented	First hot-air balloon flight	First steam railroad in use

TRAINS

When was the first passenger steam railroad?

One of the first passenger steam railroads was built by the British engineer George Stephenson in 1825. His *Locomotion* engine pulled open passenger carriages on the Stockton to Darlington Railway in England. Its top speed was just 15 miles per hour. This was much quicker than earlier railroads, where freight wagons were pulled along iron rails by horses.

BELOW George Stephenson's *Locomotion*

electric rail

concrete beam

How do monorail trains work?

Monorail trains run above or hang below a single rail or track. The earliest monorail was built in 1880. Today, most monorail trains run on wheels along the top of the concrete beam that forms the track. Guide wheels also run along the side of the beam and help to keep the train steady. Electric rails provide power and some trains operate without drivers.

TGV

What are maglev trains?

Maglev trains have no engines or wheels. They levitate, or float, just above a track. Maglev is short for 'magnetic levitation'. A powerful magnetic field is created by coils of electrically charged wire in the track. This works with strong magnets on the train to lift it up and propel it forward. Maglevs go faster than other trains because they are not slowed down by the friction caused by wheels on tracks.

ABOVE Maglevs can travel at an amazing speed of 310 miles per hour.

Where do TGV trains operate?

The streamlined TGV is France's *Train à Grande Vitesse*, which means high-speed train. These electric passenger trains run on special tracks and can travel as fast as 186 miles per hour, making them the fastest conventional trains in the world. Most high-speed trains today are pulled by powerful electric or diesel engines.

RIGHT A TGV train

The pantograph draws electrical power from an overhead wire above the track.

The TGV's onboard computer in the driver's cab controls all the train's working systems.

Electric motors power the engine's driving wheels.

DID YOU KNOW?
The world's first underground subway was opened in London, England, in 1863. Passengers travelled on the Metropolitan Line in cars pulled by steam engines.

77

TRANSPORTATION KEY DATES

7000 BC	3500 BC	AD 400	1783	1825
First dugout canoes and rafts	**First sailing boats and wheeled carts**	**Catamaran boat invented**	**First hot-air balloon flight**	**First steam railroad in use**

BOATS

How were prehistoric boats made?

The earliest boats, around 7000 BC, were simple dug-out canoes made from hollowed-out logs, or rafts built with bundles of logs or reeds tied together. In Great Britain, coracles had an oval frame made from woven strips of wood covered with animal skins. People moved their boats through the water with paddles and oars. By 3500 BC, people were building boats with skin or matting sails to catch the wind.

ABOVE Coracles had a coating of pitch to keep the joints watertight.

Who invented the catamaran?

South Indian fishermen invented the catamaran in around AD 400. Its name means "logs tied together". A catamaran yacht has two hulls connected by a deck that carries the mast. Having twin hulls means the catamaran does not capsize as easily as an ordinary boat.

RIGHT Small beach catamarans are designed for one or two people to sail for fun.

sail

mast

hull

hull

deck

DID YOU KNOW?

The hovercraft travels over water and land riding on a cushion of air. Powerful jets force air under the boat, so that it hovers just above the water. It was invented in 1959 by the British engineer Sir Christopher Sydney Cockerell.

Why are hydrofoil boats so fast?

A hydrofoil is a boat that flies across water. The boat has foils—special wing-shaped blade—attached to struts on its underside. As water rushes over the foils, the boat's hull rises up out of the water. The boat can speed along, free from the drag that affects ordinary boats. Enrico Forlanini, an Italian inventor, built the first hydrofoil in 1906.

RIGHT A hydrofoil

front foil

strut

What are jet skis?

A jet ski is a cross between a motorcycle and a boat. Its engine drives a pump that forces a jet of water out of the back of the jet ski to propel it forward. Sitting on the back of a jet ski, a rider can go fast, turn quickly, and get to places that are out of reach for bigger boats.

RIGHT Jet skiing is a popular pastime on lakes and on the ocean, where riders can speed on open stretches of water.

TRANSPORTATION KEY DATES

| 7000 BC | 3500 BC | AD 400 | 1783 | 1825 |
| First dugout canoes and rafts | First sailing boats and wheeled carts | Catamaran boat invented | First hot-air balloon flight | First steam railroad in use |

SHIPS

When were large sailing ships built?

Small boats can travel along rivers and coastlines, but large ships can venture across open oceans. Around 3000 BC, the Egyptians were building large ships with square sails attached to a mast. In the early 1800s, clipper ships with many sails were the fastest cargo ships on the sea. Today, modern tall ships from countries around the world take part in annual sailing races.

mainsails

mainmast

RIGHT Modern tall ships are rigged traditionally with square sails attached to the masts.

mizzen sails

BELOW A tourist river steamer today with a paddle in the back.

What are paddle steamers?

The first paddle steamer was built in France in 1783. The ship had a steam engine to drive two 13-foot paddle wheels on its sides, which propelled the vessel forward. Steam ships needed to carry lots of coal to fuel their engines, so ships became much bigger. In 1897, English engineer Charles Parsons tested a new steam turbine engine, which made steam ships much faster than before.

foresails

Who travels on cruise liners?

Cruise liners are floating luxury hotels for tourists. They have ballrooms, restaurants, stores, movie theaters, tennis courts and even swimming pools. Before plane travel became popular after World War II, people traveled the world in giant liners like Great Britain's *Mauretania*. This was the first cruise liner to go into service, in 1907. Today, the *Queen Mary 2* carries 2,620 passengers and a crew of 1,253.

jib

observation deck

bowsprit

BELOW The *Queen Mary 2* is the world's largest cruise liner.

passenger cabins

DID YOU KNOW?
Supertankers are the largest ships in the world. They can carry two million barrels of oil. They are so big, it can take them 6 miles to stop!

How are passenger ferries powered?

Since 1939, most modern ships, including ferries, have had diesel engines. These turn underwater propellers, which drive the ships through the water. Roll-on-roll-off ferries have built-in ramps, so that cars, trucks, and other vehicles can drive on and off easily when the ship is in port. The first such ferry ran in Scotland in 1851. It had railroad lines on board, to carry steam trains across a river.

TRANSPORTATION KEY DATES

| 7000 BC First dugout canoes and rafts | 3500 BC First sailing boats and wheeled carts | AD 400 Catamaran boat invented | 1783 First hot-air balloon flight | 1825 First steam railroad in use |

BALLOONS AND AIRSHIPS

When was the first hot-air balloon flight?

In 1783, a sheep, a dog, and a duck became the first passengers ever to take a hot-air balloon flight! French brothers, Joseph and Etienne Montgolfier, made the balloon out of silk and it flew for two miles above Paris, France. Later that year, they launched another balloon, which carried two volunteers a quarter mile up into the air.

LEFT The Montgolfiers' hot-air balloon

Why do balloons need hot air to fly?

Hot air is lighter than cool air, so it rises. The nylon envelope of a modern hot-air balloon is huge. It can hold a large amount of heated air, enough to lift the weight of a basket full of passengers. To take the balloon higher, the pilot fires a gas burner to make more hot air, which pushes the balloon upward. To go down, the pilot pulls a cord, which opens a flap at the top of the balloon and lets some hot air escape.

BELOW Hot-air balloons rely on gentle winds to blow them along.

Hot-air balloons cannot be steered, so they are not a reliable form of transportation. Today, they are mainly flown for sport.

DID YOU KNOW?
In 1999, a specially designed hot-air balloon flew nonstop round the world in just 20 days. The two pilots traveled in a tiny capsule.

envelope flap

envelope

propane gas burner

basket for carrying the pilot and passengers

What is an airship?

Airships are gigantic, torpedo-shaped balloons powered by engines. In 1852, the French engineer, Henri Giffard invented the first successful airship, driven by a steam engine. The balloon was 145 feet long and filled with hydrogen, a lighter-than-air gas. By 1930, luxury airships were carrying large numbers of passengers. However, in 1937 *The Hindenburg* caught fire near New York City. So highly flammable, hydrogen-filled airships went out of use.

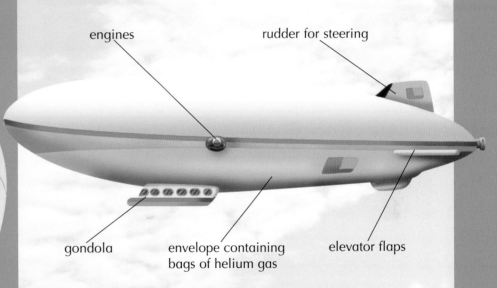

engines

rudder for steering

gondola

envelope containing bags of helium gas

elevator flaps

How do modern airships fly?

Airships have propellers and gasoline-powered engines to move them along. Pilots can change direction using a rudder and move the airship up or down by tilting elevator flaps. Passengers travel in an enclosed car, called a gondola, below the airship. Modern airships are filled with helium, a safe, lighter-than-air gas.

TRANSPORTATION KEY DATES

7000 BC	3500 BC	AD 400	1783	1825
First dugout canoes and rafts	First sailing boats and wheeled carts	Catamaran boat invented	First hot-air balloon flight	First steam railroad in use

HELICOPTERS

What is a helicopter?

A helicopter is an aircraft that has large rotating blades to lift it into the air. Helicopters can take off and land vertically, change direction quickly, hover, rotate, and even move sideways and backward in the air. Helicopters are not as safe or stable as planes, and they cannot fly as fast, but they can land in places where planes cannot go. Helicopters make ideal rescue and surveillance aircraft.

main rotor blades

covered tail rotor

ABOVE The coast guard uses helicopters for search and rescue missions at sea.

When was the helicopter invented?

In 1907, the French *Gyroplane No.1* became the first helicopter to lift off with a pilot on board. But it broke into pieces on landing. Modern helicopters are modeled on the aircraft invented by a Russian-American, Igor Sikorsky, in 1939. His design had one main set of rotor blades on top and a smaller tail rotor at the back, like helicopters today.

RIGHT Igor Sikorsky's *VS-300* helicopter

84

How does a helicopter fly?

pilot's cockpit

When a helicopter's blades rotate, they push air downward and this lifts the aircraft up. As the rotor blades turn, they also turn the helicopter body, so most helicopters have a small rotor near the tail, which turns in the opposite direction and prevents the aircraft from spinning. A pilot steers the helicopter by tilting the angle of the rotor blades forward or backward, left or right.

DID YOU KNOW?
The world's biggest helicopter is the Russian *Mil MI-26*. It's over 130 feet long, has eight blades and can carry massive loads!

Why do some helicopters have twin rotors?

The *Chinook* helicopter has one main rotor at the front and one at the back of its long, boxy fuselage, or body. The rotors spin in opposite directions to cancel each other out, making the helicopter strong and stable. *Chinook* helicopters can be loaded from either side and carry extremely heavy loads. They were first used by the US Army in 1962.

RIGHT The *Sea Knight* military helicopter also has twin rotors, but carries lighter loads than the *Chinook*.

fuselage

landing wheels

85

TRANSPORTATION KEY DATES

| 7000 BC First dugout canoes and rafts | 3500 BC First sailing boats and wheeled carts | AD 400 Catamaran boat invented | 1783 First hot-air balloon flight | 1825 First steam railroad in use |

AIRPLANES

BELOW The Wright brothers' famous *Flyer* plane of 1903

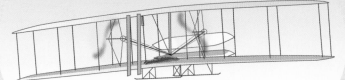

When was the first plane flight?

In 1903, two American brothers, Wilbur and Orville Wright, built the first powered airplane that flew for any distance. Their homemade aircraft had a gas engine connected to two propellers by bicycle chains. Orville controlled the plane by pulling wires that bent the fabric wings slightly. His historic first flight lasted just 12 seconds and was recorded on camera.

ABOVE Today, the gigantic 555-seat *Airbus A380* is the largest passenger plane in the sky.

How do jet planes work?

The first jet engine was built by the British engineer Frank Whittle in 1937. But Ernst Heinkel built the first jet plane in Germany, in 1939. Most airliners today are powered by fanjet engines. These have a large fan that sucks air in at the front. Some of this air is forced into a combustion chamber, where fuel is added, and burns to create hot gases. These drive the fan and blast out of the back of the engine, helping to force the airplane forward. However, most of the thrust, or forward push of the plane, comes from the air that passes around the engine.

Inside a fan-jet engine

Hot air is blasted out.

Cool air is sucked in.

combustion chamber

Some air passes around the engine, cooling it and providing most of the thrust.

Where do jump jets operate?

Most planes need a long runway to take off. Jump jets can take off with a very short run or even rise straight up into the air. The first vertical takeoff plane was the British fighter *Harrier* jump jet, built in 1966. It was designed to operate from an aircraft carrier in the ocean. The plane has four nozzles, which direct the jet engine thrust downward for vertical lift.

ABOVE Once airborne, a jump jet's nozzles turn so they can propel the plane forward.

DID YOU KNOW?
The superjumbo *Airbus A380* is so big, its tail is as high as a seven-story building and there would be room for 70 cars to park on its wings!

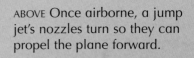
Stream-lined body shape for speed

ABOVE *Concorde* cruised at around 1,342 miles per hour—almost twice the speed of sound.

What is a supersonic plane?

A plane that flies faster than the speed of sound—761 miles per hour—is supersonic. The first plane to break the sound barrier flew in 1947, and in 1976, *Concorde* became the first supersonic jet to operate a passenger service. *Concorde*, designed by British and French engineers, stopped flying passengers in 2003.

NAVIGATION

Finding the way when traveling long distances was a problem for travelers until the invention of navigation tools. The astrolabe uses the position of the stars in the sky to navigate, and the compass uses Earth's magnetism to locate north and south. Discover who invented radar and how it helps ships avoid icebergs, how sonar works and how it is used to search for underwater objects as varied as fish, submarines, and even the Loch Ness monster! Find out how satellites circling the globe, far above us, are fast becoming invaluable navigation aids for us all.

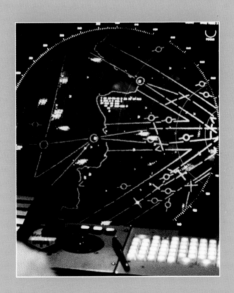

NAVIGATION KEY DATES

| AD 1100 First magnetic compass | 1470 Astrolabe adapted for use at sea | 1731 Octant invented for sea navigation | 1757 Sextant first used at sea | 1911 Ship's gyrocompass invented |

NAVIGATIONAL AIDS

A sailor's astrolabe

A rotating arm with sight holes was lined up with the Sun.

How did sailors first navigate at sea?

Navigation is all about knowing where you are and in which direction you are headed. The astrolabe was first used in around 200 BC by astronomers in Greece to locate the position of the Sun and stars. Much later, in the 1470s, it was turned into a simple navigational aid for ships at sea. Sailors used the astrolabe to measure the height of the Sun and then work out the ship's latitude—how far north or south the ship was.

pointer

circular scale

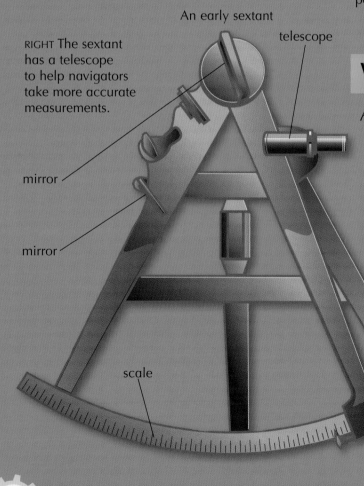

An early sextant

telescope

RIGHT The sextant has a telescope to help navigators take more accurate measurements.

mirror

mirror

scale

Who invented the sextant?

A new navigational aid, called the octant, was invented in 1731, both in England by John Hadley and in the US by Thomas Godfrey. This was a more reliable instrument for finding latitude, since its measurements were not affected by the movements of the ship. Later, in 1757, the Englishman John Campbell improved upon the octant and invented the sextant. This has twin mirrors to line up an image of the Sun, Moon, or stars with the horizon. It measures the height angle between them to calculate a ship's position at sea.

When was the compass invented?

The Earth acts like a giant magnet, with magnetic north and south poles. This makes the magnetized needle on a compass always swing into a north-south position. The first simple magnetic compasses with a hanging needle were probably used by Chinese sailors in around AD 1100. They made long-distance ocean navigation possible for the first time. Modern compasses have two or more magnetized needles that turn freely around a central point inside a container full of liquid.

needle

LEFT A modern handheld compass

DID YOU KNOW?

It's difficult to draw a map of our round world on a flat sheet of paper. In 1569, the Flemish mapmaker Gerardus Mercator worked out a way of doing this accurately enough for ships to navigate a journey around the world.

What is a gyrocompass?

The more accurate ship's gyrocompass was invented by the American Elmer Sperry, in 1911. This compass does not use magnetism to find north. It has a quickly spinning wheel, called a gyroscope, that can keep the compass needle pointing true north, however rough the seas.

RIGHT Ships today use an electronic gyrocompass to navigate at sea.

NAVIGATION KEY DATES

| AD 1100 First magnetic compass | 1470 Astrolabe adapted for use at sea | 1731 Octant invented for sea navigation | 1757 Sextant first used at sea | 1911 Ship's gyrocompass invented |

RADAR

DID YOU KNOW?
The British government originally employed Robert Alexander Watson-Watt to develop a "death ray" using radio waves to knock enemy aircraft out of the sky. He came up with radar instead.

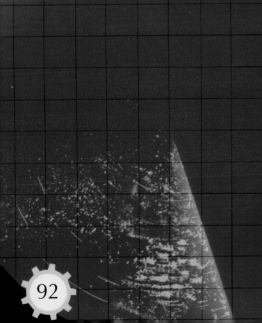

What is radar?

The word radar is short for RAdio Detection And Ranging. Radar is used to locate distant objects, such as aircraft or ships, by sending out powerful radio waves and analyzing the echoes that return. By bouncing a signal off an object, a radar system can work out exactly where that object is, how big it is, what shape it is, how fast it's moving, and in which direction it's going.

RIGHT Large radar dishes send out radio waves into the sky and can detect aircraft that are hundreds of miles away.

When was radar invented?

The first practical radar system was invented in 1935 by the Scottish physicist Robert Alexander Watson-Watt. A few years earlier, he had developed a way of using radio signals to track the movements of thunderstorms. During World War II, Watson-Watt's radar defense system was used to detect the approach of enemy aircraft and give an early warning of bombing raids.

LEFT Weather forecasters use radar screens to track the movements of rainstorms.

1915
First sonar
detection device

1935
Radar invented
to detect aircraft

1978
GPS becomes the first satellite
navigation system in operation

2005
Launch of the first Galileo
navigation satellites

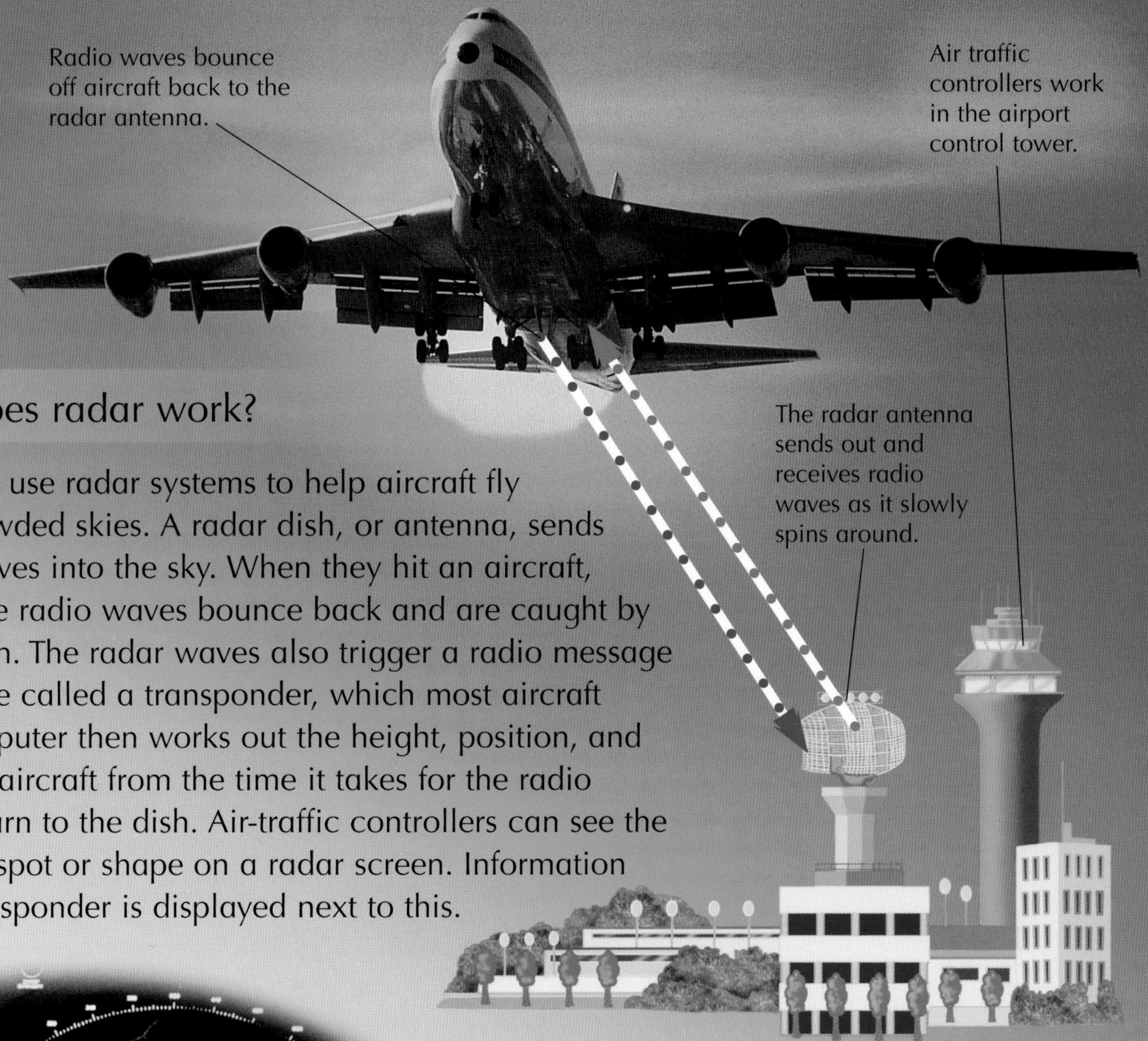

Radio waves bounce
off aircraft back to the
radar antenna.

Air traffic
controllers work
in the airport
control tower.

The radar antenna
sends out and
receives radio
waves as it slowly
spins around.

How does radar work?

Busy airports use radar systems to help aircraft fly
safely in crowded skies. A radar dish, or antenna, sends
out radio waves into the sky. When they hit an aircraft,
some of these radio waves bounce back and are caught by
the radar dish. The radar waves also trigger a radio message
from a device called a transponder, which most aircraft
carry. A computer then works out the height, position, and
speed of the aircraft from the time it takes for the radio
waves to return to the dish. Air-traffic controllers can see the
aircraft as a spot or shape on a radar screen. Information
from the transponder is displayed next to this.

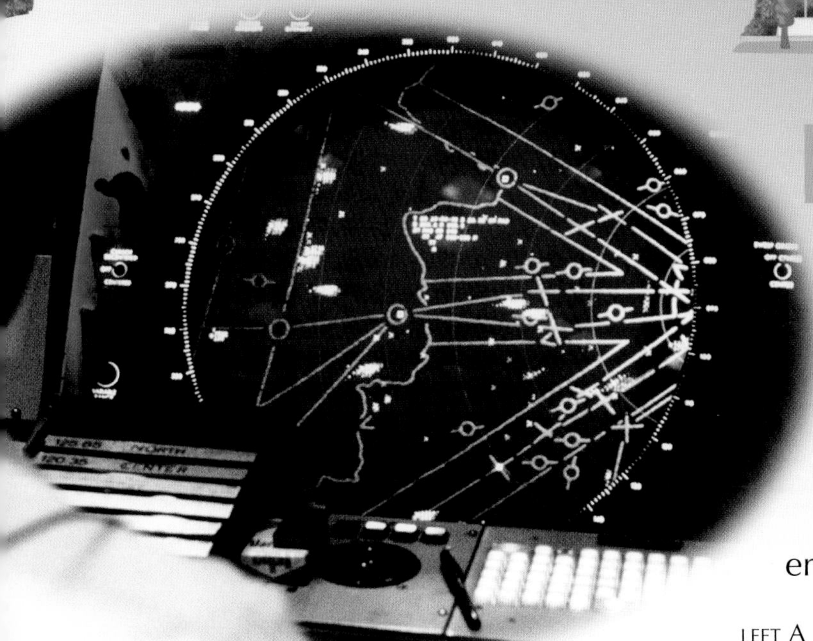

Who uses radar today?

Radar is widely used today as a navigation
instrument. Air traffic controllers monitor
and guide air traffic using radar. Ships
use it to find their way at sea, especially
in bad weather or at night, and to avoid
hazards such as other ships, rocks, or
icebergs. The military uses radar to locate
enemy forces and to aim or detect missiles.

LEFT A radar screen

93

NAVIGATION KEY DATES

| AD **1100** First magnetic compass | **1470** Astrolabe adapted for use at sea | **1731** Octant invented for sea navigation | **1757** Sextant first used at sea | **1911** Ship's gyrocompass invented |

SONAR

What is sonar?

The word sonar stands for SOund NAvigation and Ranging. Sonar uses underwater sound waves to locate shipwrecks, rocks, and other ocean features that could be a hazard to ships at sea. Chart makers also use sonar information to create accurate maps of the ocean floor, which help ships to navigate safely.

LEFT Sonar devices help ships to detect underwater hazards, such as the parts of icebergs hidden beneath the ocean's surface.

BELOW Military ships use towed sonar devices to detect and track the movements of enemy submarines.

Why was sonar invented?

A sonar listening device for detecting submarines was first invented in 1915, during World War I, by the French physicist Paul Langevin. Scientists knew that sound waves, unlike light or radio waves, can travel at high speed and for long distances through water. This made them ideal for probing the ocean depths to locate and track enemy vessels.

94

A sonar transponder measures the time it takes for a sound wave to travel down to the seabed and bounce back again.

Sound waves are sent out by the ship.

Echoes bounce back from the shipwreck on the seabed.

How does sonar work?

A special sonar device, called a transponder, is attached to the hull of a ship. The transponder sends out regular beats of high-pitched sounds every second. These sound waves travel down through the water and when they hit the seabed, or an underwater object such as a shipwreck, they bounce back as echoes. The transponder records the time taken for the echoes to return to the ship. An onboard computer then uses this information to calculate the shipwreck's depth and distance from the ship.

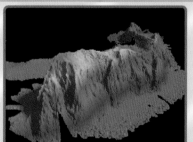

BELOW A 3D sonar image of an underwater mountain

Who uses sonar?

Sonar transponders send the results of sonar surveys to a computer, which analyzes and then displays the information on a monitor screen. Fishermen use simple sonar displays, which can measure the depth of the seabed and the location of shoals of fish. Ocean chart makers use multibeam sonar devices. These send sound waves straight down, forward, and also to the side to create three-dimensional (3-D) maps of features on the ocean floor.

DID YOU KNOW?
In 2003, a British television documentary used 600 separate sonar beams to survey Loch Ness in Scotland. The goal was to prove that Nessie, the Loch Ness monster, does not exist!

NAVIGATION KEY DATES

AD 1100	1470	1731	1757	1911
First magnetic compass	Astrolabe adapted for use at sea	Octant invented for sea navigation	Sextant first used at sea	Ship's gyrocompass invented

SATELLITE NAVIGATION

What is satellite navigation?

Satellite navigation uses radio signals from a network of satellites circling the Earth in space to work out the exact position of an electronic receiver anywhere on the planet. The best-known satellite navigation system is the Global Positioning System, or GPS for short. The US Air Force developed the GPS satellite network in 1978 to enable it to target its war missiles accurately. Today, the US Department of Defense still controls the GPS network, but the technology can be used by anyone free of charge. In 2005, the European Union started launching its own GPS satellites for a new network called Galileo.

DID YOU KNOW?
Some cell phones have GPS technology, which shows an on-screen route map to a destination. It's possible to view and listen to step-by-step directions, just using the handset.

Each satellite transmits radio signals from space giving its position and the exact time that the signal was sent.

How does GPS work?

The GPS network uses 24 solar-powered satellites that circle the Earth at a height of about 12,000 miles. These satellites carry highly accurate atomic clocks and transmit radio signals that can be picked up by the antennas of GPS receivers on Earth. The receiver compares how long it takes for the signals from four different satellites to reach it and uses this information to calculate its exact position.

Who uses GPS navigation?

GPS navigation is widely used today by people traveling in cars, ships, and airplanes. In-car navigation systems can show or tell drivers the exact roads to take to a specific address. A computerized map is displayed on a screen positioned within easy sight on the dashboard. Handheld GPS receivers are ideal for mountain climbers and hikers who are traveling in remote areas. Talking GPS systems are also being developed to provide navigation assistance for blind people.

The receiver on this boat calculates its position by comparing the distance to four different satellites.

RIGHT The arrows on a moving map point to where the car is and show the direction in which the driver wants to travel.

Why do fishermen use GPS?

Many fishermen plan a fishing trip by looking at maps and charts to work out fish migration routes and likely feeding grounds. If they plot these locations using GPS equipment, it can direct them right there, even in bad weather or thick fog. Once fishermen find a good fishing spot, they can also save the exact location on their GPS equipment, instead of using marker buoys that would alert other fishermen to the site.

LEFT GPS uses signals from four different satellites to pinpoint locations.

97

SPACE

From our first glimpses of space through early telescopes to space travel today, inventions have been the only way that we could find out more about the universe beyond our planet. Discover where the Hubble Telescope is, how rockets fly, and why satellites can stay in orbit around the Earth. Learn about astronauts who space-walk in the empty weightlessness of outer space around their space shuttles, or live in space stations for months at a time. Read about the space probes traveling into deep space to investigate parts of the universe never before explored.

SPACE KEY DATES

AD 1608	1926	1957	1961	1962
First successful refracting telescope	Liquid-fuel rocket invented	Rocket took the first satellite into space	First successful space capsule	First space probe to reach another planet

TELESCOPES

Who first invented the telescope?

The Dutch spectacle maker Hans Lippershey made the first successful refracting telescope in 1608. He realized that by looking through two lenses, placed at each end of a tube, far-away objects appeared larger. By 1609, the Italian scientist Galileo Galilei was using a similar telescope to study the night sky. He used it to map the surface of the Moon and discover the planet Jupiter's four moons.

LEFT Galileo Galilei at his telescope

How does a reflecting telescope work?

A reflecting telescope uses mirrors to help astronomers see a brighter and clearer view of distant stars and planets. The English scientist Isaac Newton designed and built the first reflecting telescope in 1668. The telescope collects light rays from an object on a curved mirror at one end. The mirror reflects, or bounces, the rays onto a flat, angled mirror to form an image. A lens then magnifies this image in the viewing eyepiece.

RIGHT Newton's reflecting telescope

DID YOU KNOW?
Some of the largest reflecting telescopes in the world are on the island of Hawaii, USA. The twin 30-foot Keck telescopes sit over 13,000 feet high on top of Mauna Kea, an extinct volcano.

lens

eyepiece

curved mirror

light rays

Inside a reflecting telescope

flat, angled mirror

What is a radio telescope?

Astronomers use a radio telescope linked to computers to detect radio waves and create pictures of distant space objects. In addition to radio waves, space objects such as black holes and galaxies also give out gamma rays, infra-red, ultraviolet, and X-rays, which people cannot see. These can be detected by special kinds of telescope. The atmosphere blocks out most of these waves, so they are usually observed from artificial satellites, above the atmosphere.

antenna

ABOVE The Arecibo radio telescope in Puerto Rico has a single, giant dish. This collects and directs radio waves from space onto a receiving antenna.

Where is the Hubble telescope?

In 1990, the *Hubble* telescope was launched 373 miles into space. It still circles the Earth today. This huge space telescope works in the same way as ordinary reflecting telescopes, but it can see much more clearly. From beyond the Earth's atmosphere, it can take sharp pictures of the universe over 12 billion light-years away. Hubble has helped astronomers to make incredible discoveries about black holes and how stars are formed and die.

ABOVE *Hubble* space telescope

RIGHT A spiral galaxy of stars viewed by *Hubble*

101

SPACE KEY DATES

| AD 1608 | 1926 | 1957 | 1961 | 1962 |
| First successful refracting telescope | Liquid-fuel rocket invented | Rocket took the first satellite into space | First successful space capsule | First space probe to reach another planet |

ROCKETS

LEFT Rockets transport astronauts, satellites, or research equipment into space.

When were rockets first built?

The first gunpowder rockets were made by the Chinese around 1,000 years ago and used as fireworks or weapons. In 1926, the American scientist Robert Goddard built the first controllable rocket that ran on liquid fuel— a mixture of gasoline and oxygen.

The launchpad scaffolding supports the rocket until liftoff.

What is a space rocket?

A space rocket is a high-speed, cylinder-shaped engine powerful enough to overcome the pull of Earth's gravity and carry objects into space. Space rockets need to carry enormous tanks of fuel. The burning fuel produces a jet of hot waste gases that lifts the rocket off the ground. The first rocket powerful enough to reach space was a weapon invented by the German engineer Werhner von Braun in 1942.

BELOW Von Braun's unmanned *V-2* rocket missile was used to bomb Britain during World War II.

How do rockets fly?

When you blow up a balloon, then let it go without tying the end, the balloon is thrust forward by the escaping jet of air. This is how a rocket flies into space. A rocket burns fuel with liquid oxygen to make a powerful jet of very hot exhaust gases. This shoots out of the bottom of the rocket, lifting it into the air at high speed.

The pointed nose cone cuts through the air.

The payload is what the rocket is designed to carry—the cargo and astronauts.

rocket guidance system

liquid fuel tank

liquid oxygen tank

pumps

The combustion engine is where the fuel burns.

exhaust nozzles

The tail fins keep the rocket stable during flight.

BELOW Space rockets are made up of a number of different stages, which fall away once the fuel is used up.

DID YOU KNOW?
Saturn V, which carried the US's *Apollo* spacecraft to the Moon, was one of the biggest rockets ever to be invented. It was as tall as a 30-story skyscraper and as powerful as 150 jumbo jets.

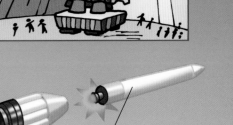

Stage three carries the payload into orbit. Once the satellite or spacecraft is launched, the rocket's work is done.

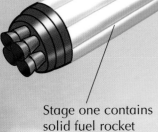

Stage two engines then take over. They burn liquid fuel, which thrusts the rocket upward.

Stage one contains solid fuel rocket boosters, which burn to give liftoff.

Who sent the first rocket into orbit?

The first rocket to put an object into orbit was launched by the Soviet Union in 1957. It carried the first space satellite, called *Sputnik 1*. In the 1960s, Soviet and American scientists developed multistage rockets. These carried manned spacecraft into orbit around the Earth. They were made up of several different sections. Each had its own engine and a fuel and oxygen supply, which enabled the rockets to travel farther into space.

SPACE KEY DATES

AD 1608	1926	1957	1961	1962
First successful refracting telescope	Liquid-fuel rocket invented	Rocket took the first satellite into space	First successful space capsule	First space probe to reach another planet

SATELLITES

When was the first satellite invented?

A satellite is anything that orbits, or circles, a larger object in space, such as the Moon orbiting the Earth. But the first artificial satellite, called *Sputnik I,* was invented by Soviet scientists in 1957. Once in orbit, this simple satellite measured the temperature of the Earth's atmosphere. It sent back the information using radio signals.

ABOVE RIGHT
Sputnik I satellite

DID YOU KNOW?
Old satellites and discarded rocket parts are left to float around in space. Scientists estimate that there are now around 70,000 pieces of "space junk" orbiting the Earth.

BELOW The speed of the moving satellite balances the downward pull of gravity to keep it in orbit.

Why do satellites stay in orbit?

Most satellites move in almost circular orbits a few hundred miles above the Earth. Gravity is almost as strong there as it is at the surface, and pulls the satellite downward. The satellite is constantly falling toward the center of the Earth. But because of its sideways motion, and the curvature of the Earth, the satellite circles the planet at the same height. Even satellites thousands of miles above the Earth are held in orbit by the Earth's gravity.

How do satellites work?

Most satellites are powered by solar panels, which convert sunlight into electricity. Small rocket thrusters move and turn the satellites. Sensors check that they are facing in the right direction. All satellites have communication antennas, radio receivers, and transmitters to receive signals and send messages to ground stations back on Earth. Satellites also carry specific instruments, depending on the job they are intended to do.

BELOW Ground stations send and receive signals from large dishes pointed at satellites in space.

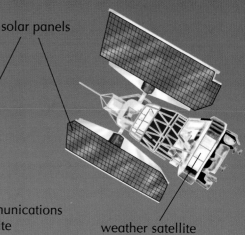

solar panels

communications satellite

weather satellite

radio receiver and transmitter

communication antenna

RIGHT A weather satellite has onboard cameras to take photographs of cloud formations, such as this hurricane. These are sent to weather-forecasting stations back on Earth.

What are satellites used for?

There are several different kinds of satellites in space, each doing different jobs. In addition to weather satellites, there are communication satellites, which broadcast television and telephone signals all over the world. Some satellites send back photographs, which are used to make maps. Others provide information about the Earth and the universe to help with scientific investigations. Navigation satellites help people to find their way and pinpoint exact locations on Earth.

SPACE KEY DATES

AD 1608	1926	1957	1961	1962
First successful refracting telescope	Liquid-fuel rocket invented	Rocket took the first satellite into space	First successful space capsule	First space probe to reach another planet

SPACECRAFT

RIGHT Yuri Gagarin traveled once around the Earth in the space capsule *Vostok I*. His flight took almost two hours.

What is a space capsule?

A space capsule is a spacecraft designed to carry astronauts. It is launched into space on a rocket. For the return journey, the capsule has a heat shield. This protects the astronauts from high temperatures as they reenter the Earth's atmosphere at great speed. The capsule uses parachutes to slow down and land or splash down in the sea. The Soviet Union built the first successful space capsule in 1961. It carried the Russian astronaut Yuri Gagarin. He was the first person ever to see the planet Earth from space.

Which spacecraft first landed on the Moon?

In 1969, American astronauts were carried to the Moon in the *Apollo 11* spacecraft. Neil Armstrong and Edwin "Buzz" Aldrin, left the spacecraft orbiting the Moon and traveled down to land on the Moon's surface in a small lunar module.

BELOW Armstrong and Aldrin were the first men ever to walk on the Moon.

DID YOU KNOW?
Scientists invented special protective suits for the Space Shuttle astronauts to use when 'space walking'. They wear them outside the spacecraft when repairing satellites or servicing the Hubble space telescope.

lunar module

The Shuttle orbiter carries the crew and cargo into space and brings them back to Earth. It is used for several space missions.

Why was the Space Shuttle invented?

Space Shuttles were designed as the first reusable spacecraft. A space capsule transported by rocket can only be used on one journey. But Space Shuttles transport astronauts and science equipment into space to carry out investigations or launch satellites, then they fly back to Earth to be used again. The US launched the first Space Shuttle, *Columbia*, in 1981.

The external fuel tank burns up after use and cannot be reused.

BELOW The Space Shuttle is launched into space like a rocket. It acts like a spacecraft in space, then glides back to Earth like an airplane.

Two solid-fuel rocket boosters are used for liftoff and then recycled for use in other missions.

How is the Space Shuttle reused?

New fuel tanks are added to a Space Shuttle on each new mission. At liftoff, two solid-fuel rocket boosters launch the Shuttle orbiter. Once this fuel is used up, the rocket boosters fall away and parachute into the ocean. These are collected and used again. The liquid fuel tank comes away later, but burns up in Earth's atmosphere. The Shuttle carries the astronauts and equipment into orbit where it circles the Earth. On its return journey, the Shuttle lands like a giant airplane on a runway.

107

SPACE KEY DATES

AD 1608	1926	1957	1961	1962
First successful refracting telescope	Liquid-fuel rocket invented	Rocket took the first satellite into space	First successful space capsule	First space probe to reach another planet

SPACE STATIONS

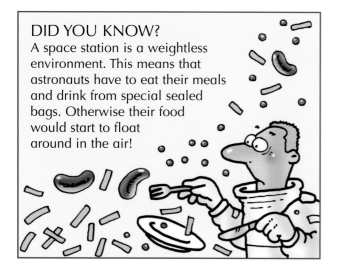

DID YOU KNOW?
A space station is a weightless environment. This means that astronauts have to eat their meals and drink from special sealed bags. Otherwise their food would start to float around in the air!

Who launched the first space station?

In 1971, the Soviet Union launched the first-ever space station, *Salyut 1*. This research laboratory was designed to remain in space, orbiting the Earth. Three astronauts traveled up to the station in the spacecraft *Soyuz II*. The crew set the first space duration record by staying onboard for 22 days. After five months in space, the station fell back to Earth and burned up as it reentered the Earth's atmosphere.

BELOW *Soyuz II* docking with *Salyut 1*

How many space stations have there been?

The Russians put six successful *Salyut* stations into orbit between 1971 and 1982. *Skylab* was launched by the US in 1973. In 1986, the Russians launched a larger space station called *Mir*. All these space stations have since either fallen back to Earth or been removed from orbit at the end of their use.

RIGHT The US's Space Shuttle *Atlantis* docks with Russia's *Mir* space station.

solar panels

research laboratory

ABOVE Planned for completion in 2010, the ISS will be the biggest space station ever built.

RIGHT Scientists from different countries carry out experiments in the research laboratories of the International Space Station.

What is the ISS?

In 1998, several countries worked together to design the International Space Station, or ISS. The ISS is so big it has to be built in sections and assembled out in space by astronauts. The station has huge, wing-shaped solar panels, which collect energy from the Sun to power all the onboard machines. There is a generator for making oxygen, so that the astronauts can breathe and there are systems to clean and purify the water. Spacecraft delivering new crew members, supplies, and equipment link up with the station at docking ports.

BELOW An astronaut "space walking".

Why were space stations invented?

Astronauts carry out scientific research in laboratories on board space stations. From space, it is easier to study the universe and observe the Earth's weather systems. Some scientists investigate how the human body is affected by living in a weightless environment, where astronauts and objects float around inside the space station. Scientists also test materials that might one day be used to build spacecraft to carry people to other planets, like Mars.

109

SPACE KEY DATES

AD 1608	1926	1957	1961	1962
First successful	Liquid-fuel rocket	Rocket took the first	First successful	First space probe to
refracting telescope	invented	satellite into space	space capsule	reach another planet

SPACE PROBES

Who built the first space probe?

The Russian *Lunik I* was the first space probe
to be launched in 1959, but it failed to
reach its target, the Moon. Space probes are
unmanned spacecraft that are launched deep
into space. They either fly past, orbit, or land
on planets and collect information about
them. In 1962, the US's *Mariner 2* probe flew
by Venus, making it the first spacecraft to
encounter another planet successfully.

RIGHT The *Mariner 2* space probe
investigated the planet Venus.

Venus

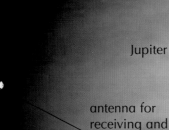

Jupiter

antenna for
receiving and
transmitting
data

Why do we need space probes?

Space probes are loaded with high-tech
equipment and scientific instruments to
gather data on distant planets. Once the
spacecraft reach their target planet, the
equipment switches on. It starts to take
accurate pictures, record measurements,
and collect mapping information, which
is transmitted back to scientists on Earth.
Aside from Pluto—the farthest planet from
the Sun—all of the planets in our solar
system have now been explored.

LEFT The *Voyager 2* is the only space probe
to have flown past four different planets
—Jupiter, Saturn, Uranus, and Neptune.

What is the *Cassini-Huygens* probe?

The *Cassini-Huygens* space probe was launched in 1997 to investigate the planet Saturn. The spacecraft reached Saturn's orbit in 2004. From here, *Cassini* began a four-year study of the planet, its atmosphere, its rings, and many moons. The smaller probe, *Huygens*, was later released by the main spacecraft. It successfully landed on Titan, Saturn's largest moon.

BELOW The *Cassini-Huygens* space probe is one of the largest ever built. It's about as big as a 30-seater bus.

Saturn

Neptune

How far can space probes travel?

Since there are no astronauts on board, scientists can risk sending probes out into deep space to investigate unknown parts of the universe. The first space probe to leave our solar system was *Pioneer 10,* in 1983. Space probes such as this travel for many years and for millions of miles into outer space. No one really knows what they may discover there in the future.

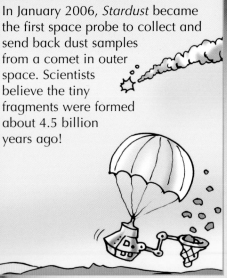

DID YOU KNOW?
In January 2006, *Stardust* became the first space probe to collect and send back dust samples from a comet in outer space. Scientists believe the tiny fragments were formed about 4.5 billion years ago!

Uranus

111

WEAPONS

Since wooden bows and arrows were invented, weapons have come a long way. Machine guns and laser-guided missiles are just some of the weapons, military equipment, and machines that have been developed for warfare. Find out when bullet-proof vests were invented and how bombs can prevent floods. Discover why tanks have caterpillar tracks, which warplanes can fly without a pilot, how many planes an aircraft carrier can hold, and the smart technology modern torpedoes use to locate their targets.

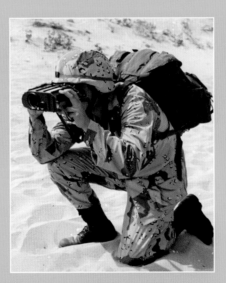

WEAPONS KEY DATES

| 1400 BC Oldest-known armor worn by soldiers | 400 BC Wooden crossbow invented | AD 1250 Longbow invented for warfare | 1350 Hand cannons first developed | 1500 First sailing warships |

BOWS AND ARROWS

boulders

ABOVE A Roman catapult used a throwing arm to fire boulders.

What were the first weapons used for?

The first simple weapons made by ancient peoples were used for hunting. In around 400,000 BC, people in Europe were making sharpened wooden spears to hunt huge mammoths. By 30,000 BC, hunters in Africa had invented the bow and arrow to kill animals that were out of reach of their spears. One early weapon that was used in battle, was a kind of giant catapult with a tightened bowstring for firing rocks instead of arrows. In around 400 BC, Greek and Roman soldiers used these wooden catapults to fling boulders at enemies up to 1,000 feet away.

Where was the longbow invented?

The longbow was invented in Wales, UK, during the 13th century. This longer version of the traditional short bow was a more powerful weapon, capable of shooting arrows greater distances— up to 650 feet. In battle, archers could load their longbows quickly to send storms of arrows raining down on their enemies.

LEFT An archer today using a replica longbow. When held upright, a wooden longbow stands as tall as the person who fires it.

DID YOU KNOW?

When under fire in battle, groups of Roman soldiers locked their shields together to defend themselves against arrows. This tactic was known as the tortoise formation.

RIGHT The crossbow is a powerful long-range weapon.

When was the crossbow invented?

The first crossbows were wooden and made in Greece in around 400 BC. Archers rested the end of the weapon on the ground to fire it. Since the 15th century, the crossbow has been held and aimed like a rifle, with the weapon resting on the archer's shoulder. Modern crossbows are mostly constructed from fiberglass and they shoot aluminum arrows called bolts.

How does a crossbow fire bolts?

A crossbow works just like a bow and arrow held on its side. As the bowstring is pulled back tightly, it stores up energy, which is used to fire bolts. First, the string is locked in position by a latch. Next, the bolt is put on the track ready to fire. Once the bolt is set, the archer looks through the sight to take aim and presses on the trigger to release the bowstring, which shoots the bolt at the target.

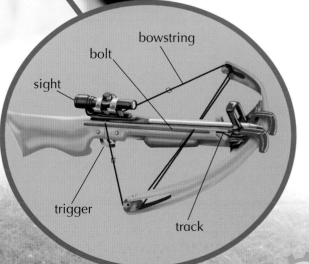

bowstring

bolt

sight

trigger

track

WEAPONS KEY DATES

| 1400 BC
Oldest-known armor
worn by soldiers | 400 BC
Wooden crossbow
invented | AD 1250
Longbow invented
for warfare | 1350
Hand cannons first
developed | 1500
First sailing
warships |

GUNS

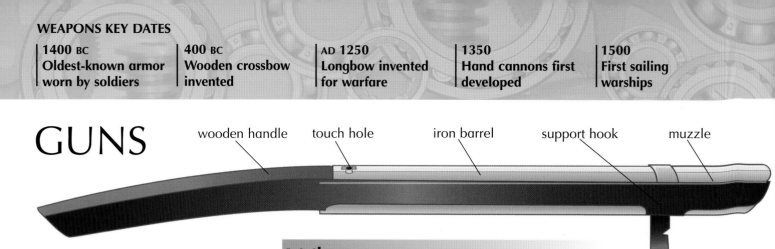

wooden handle · touch hole · iron barrel · support hook · muzzle

When were guns first invented?

The earliest guns, called hand cannons, were developed in Europe around 1350, after the discovery of gunpowder in China in AD 950. They were light enough to carry, but often too big and heavy to hold and fire without propping up the muzzle end. Hand cannons were loaded by pouring gunpowder into the barrel, then pushing in a round stone or a lead ball, called shot. A soldier fired his weapon by lighting the gunpowder with a hot wire through a touch hole in the barrel, which exploded the shot out of the gun.

What is a rifle?

A rifle is a long-barreled gun that is fired from the shoulder. It has a spiral groove within its barrel to make bullets spin when fired and hit targets more accurately over long distances. The rifle was invented in the 15th century, when the idea of "rifling"—putting grooves in the barrel—came from archers who knew that twisting an arrow's tail feathers improved its aim.

LEFT Originally, rifles were used only as military weapons. Today, many are used for hunting or in shooting competitions.

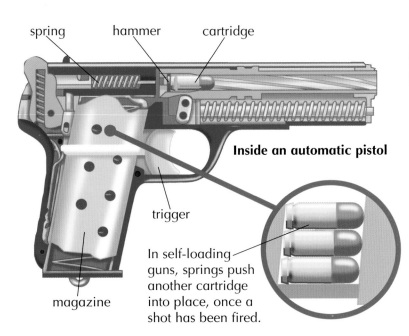

spring   hammer   cartridge

Inside an automatic pistol

trigger

In self-loading guns, springs push another cartridge into place, once a shot has been fired.

magazine

How do modern guns work?

Modern handheld guns, like this automatic pistol, can fire several cartridges quickly from a detachable box called a magazine. A cartridge is a case containing both the bullet and gunpowder together. Pulling the trigger of a gun releases a spring, which drives a hammer forward into the explosive cap at the base of the cartridge. This ignites the gunpowder, which explodes, shooting the bullet out of the gun at high speed.

Who invented the machine gun?

The water-cooled machine gun was first built in 1884 by Hiram Maxim in the US. His invention brought a huge change to warfare during World War I. This deadly weapon used the force of the gun recoiling, or jerking backward after firing a bullet, to eject the spent cartridge and reload another. As machine guns reloaded automatically, soldiers could rapidly fire a spray of bullets just by holding down the trigger. Many machine guns use ammunition belts, which are a long string of cartridges that feed quickly through the gun. The empty shells drop to the ground as soon as the bullets have been fired.

DID YOU KNOW?
Many police forces around the world now use taser guns to stun and catch criminals. These guns shoot two darts on cables that give someone a short electric shock on impact.

117

WEAPONS KEY DATES

| 1400 BC | 400 BC | AD 1250 | 1350 | 1500 |
| Oldest-known armor worn by soldiers | Wooden crossbow invented | Longbow invented for warfare | Hand cannons first developed | First sailing warships |

ARMOR

Why did soldiers first wear armor?

Soldiers first started wearing tough body armor to protect themselves against blows from sharp swords, spears, and arrows. The first armor worn by Chinese soldiers in around 1110 BC was made from thick rhino skin. By the 14th century, medieval knights in Europe were wearing heavy metal helmets and body armor made up of shaped steel plates attached by leather straps and buckles. The joints in the armor plates were protected by chain mail. This was metal cloth made from hundreds of small iron rings linked together with a leather backing.

DID YOU KNOW?
A knight's armor was very heavy, weighing about 65 pounds, and could make the wearer incredibly hot when fighting.

LEFT A medieval knight and his horse dressed ready for battle in metal armor.

BELOW Speeding bullets are flattened and slowed down in the many layers of a bullet-proof vest, which is reinforced with metal or ceramic plates.

When was the bullet-proof vest invented?

Body armor was heavy and clumsy until in 1971 the DuPont chemical company developed a special material called Kevlar for use in bullet-proof vests. Kevlar is a kind of flexible plastic that is five times stronger than the same weight of steel. Modern body armor protects police officers or soldiers against injury from knife attacks or gun fire. Protective vests prevent people from being killed by bullets, but they still suffer bruises.

protective hood

gas mask

gloves

What are chemical warfare protection suits?

Chemical warfare protection suits are worn by soldiers against possible poisonous gas, chemical, or biological attacks. These full body suits are made from special lightweight fabric that prevents chemicals or gases from passing through. Soldiers also need to wear a gas mask, which has a respirator to filter out dangerous chemicals or gases, but still allows them to breathe.

LEFT Soldiers wear full-body protection suits when under the threat of a chemical or biological attack.

BELOW Air force firemen wear fire protection suits when dealing with burning planes after a bomb attack.

How do fire protection suits work?

Fire protection suits are designed to protect people fighting fires close-up. They cover a firefighter's whole body and are made of fire-resistant fabric that stops flames and heat from burning the skin. The mask protects the face from smoke and fumes. These suits can be heavy, making firefighters' jobs even tougher when they have to climb ladders, carry away injured people, and lift heavy hoses.

WEAPONS KEY DATES

1400 BC	400 BC	AD 1250	1350	1500
Oldest-known armor worn by soldiers	Wooden crossbow invented	Longbow invented for warfare	Hand cannons first developed	First sailing warships

BOMBS

What is a bomb?

A bomb is a container of explosive material with a device, called a detonator or fuse, to set it alight. Bombs are designed to be dropped from aircraft and explode when they hit the ground. Austria dropped the first aerial bombs from unmanned, hot-air balloons in 1849. Fifty years later, during World War I, the German forces carried out aerial bombing raids on Britain from *Zeppelin* airships.

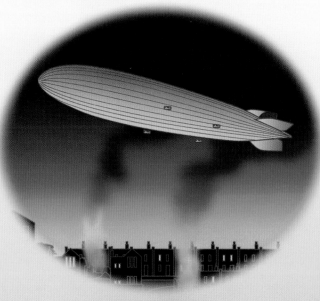

ABOVE *Zeppelin* bombers often missed their intended military targets.

BELOW Modern missiles are guided to home in accurately on targets.

When were guided missiles invented?

At the end of World War II, Germany used *V-2* rocket bombs. The *V-2* climbed to the edge of space until its engine cut out and then traveled in a huge curved path, like a thrown ball. Guided missiles are more like small unmanned planes. They are directed to their target by an onboard computer map. Shoulder-fired missile launchers have been made since the 1960s. These fire a single rocket that uses infra-red sensors to follow the heat from an enemy aircraft's engine and hit it.

1624
Submarine first
built and tested

1915
First specially built
fighter plane

1916
Battle tank
invented

1945
Atomic bomb first
used in war

1981
Stealth bomber
flies

Who invented the atomic bomb?

During World War II, scientists from the USA and Great Britain created an atomic bomb. The team was led by the American nuclear physicist J. Robert Oppenheimer. The first atomic bomb was dropped on the Japanese city of Hiroshima on the August 6, 1945, killing 80,000 people. Three days later, another atomic bomb was dropped on Nagasaki, killing about 70,000 people. Many tens of thousands from the two cities died later from cancers and sicknesses caused by radiation from the explosions. This weapon of mass destruction brought the war to an end, but at a terrible price.

RIGHT A mushroom cloud was produced by the explosion of an atomic bomb.

DID YOU KNOW?
Bombs are sometimes dropped on ice dams that form across large rivers in freezing winters. The airstrikes break up the blockage to prevent serious flooding.

How do smart bombs work?

Smart bombs are laser-guided missiles that are designed to make more accurate strikes and reduce the risk of killing innocent people. Bomber pilots in aircraft, or troops on the ground, shine a beam of laser light onto a target to guide the missiles to the right destination. Once the laser is locked in position, the missile can pinpoint its target and can even follow a target that moves.

An aircraft releases the missile into the area of reflected laser light.

Ground troops shine a laser light onto the bombing target.

121

WEAPONS KEY DATES

| **1400 BC** | **400 BC** | **AD 1250** | **1350** | **1500** |
| Oldest-known armor worn by soldiers | Wooden crossbow invented | Longbow invented for warfare | Hand cannons first developed | First sailing warships |

TANKS

When were armored tanks first made?

The British invented the first battle tank in 1916, as a secret weapon during World War I. The factory workers making the metal bodies were told they were building "water carriers" for the army, so they nicknamed the vehicles "tanks". The first tanks were covered in iron plates held together with rivets and ran on tractor engines, which were very slow. These heavy, armored vehicles were designed to move on caterpillar tracks over rough ground and were armed with powerful guns.

Why were tanks invented?

The use of the machine gun on the battlefields of World War I meant that the infantry, or foot soldiers, were easily shot down by enemy fire. Armored tanks were invented to combat this deadly weapon. Tank crews were able to advance on the enemy in safety and cross trenches, crush barbed wire, and destroy enemy machine-gun posts, clearing a path for the infantry that followed.

DID YOU KNOW?
Early tanks gave the crew inside such a bumpy ride that the soldiers had to wear padded clothing to keep from getting covered in bruises.

ABOVE The first tank was known as the *Centipede*.

RIGHT Metal caterpillar tracks can climb over all kinds of obstacles.

BELOW Troops travel safe from bullets and ambush inside the APC.

How do modern tanks work?

Modern battle tanks are heavy, armored fighting vehicles with powerful engines. They can move at speeds of up to 60 miles per hour over all kinds of terrain. Tanks are covered in thick steel to protect them against enemy fire and mines, and are strong enough to break through barricades. They are armed with either a powerful gun that fires missiles or a flame-thrower that shoots jets of burning liquid.

Inside a tank

The gun loader operates the main gun and radio communications.

What are APCs?

Armored Personnel Carriers, or APCs for short, are designed to transport troops safely to the battlefield. These light armored vehicles can carry up to 10 soldiers at a time across rough ground or through water. Most APCs are armed with just a heavy machine gun, since they are not intended as attack vehicles.

The main missile-firing gun and machine gun are located in a rotating turret.

The driver sits inside the tank beneath the turret.

123

WEAPONS KEY DATES

| **1400 BC** | **400 BC** | **AD 1250** | **1350** | **1500** |
| Oldest-known armor worn by soldiers | Wooden crossbow invented | Longbow invented for warfare | Hand cannons first developed | First sailing warships |

WARPLANES

When were fighter planes first built?

The first fighter plane was the *Fokker E. I* of 1915. Built by Germany during World War I, it was armed with machine guns. The plane was specially designed so that the guns could shoot bullets between the spinning blades of its propellers. The *Fokker D. VII* of 1918 could maneuver better.

ABOVE *Fokker D. VII*

DID YOU KNOW?
The world's heaviest bomber is the US *Boeing B-52 Stratofortress*. This enormous, long-distance aircraft is powered by eight fanjet engines. It carries loads up to one-and-a-half times its own weight.

Why were fighter planes invented?

Fighter jets were invented to attack other planes in the air, while bomber planes fired on targets on the ground. During World War II, aircraft like the powerful British *Spitfire* and the German jet-powered *Messerschmidt* became a vital part of armed combat for the first time. Today's fighter jets are relatively small and capable of maneuvering and changing direction very rapidly. The best can fly faster than the speed of sound.

LEFT A group of US fighter planes—*F/A-18C Hornets*— flying together in formation.

How do stealth planes work?

The first stealth plane, designed to be invisible to enemy radar, flew in 1981. The US *Lockheed F-117A Nighthawk* stealth fighter could fly over enemy territory and drop bombs without being seen and intercepted by enemy aircraft. Stealth planes are built in flattened shapes out of special materials that soak up radar waves instead of reflecting them. They also have cool, hidden engines that cannot be detected by heat-sensing equipment.

BELOW Stealth bombers carry their weapons on the inside to reduce their chances of being spotted by enemy radar.

Stealth planes are painted dark colors so that they can't be seen at night.

Many fighter jets are single-seaters, with room for just a pilot.

Fighter jets are usually armed with missiles and use radar to locate their targets.

What are UAVs?

Unmanned aerial vehicles, called UAVs for short, are warplanes that are either radio-controlled by operators based in ground stations, or are self-piloted. These aircraft follow computerized maps and use satellite navigation systems to reach their targets. The first UAVs were built in the 1950s for surveillance and carried cameras, sensors, and other communications equipment. Today's UAVs are also used as combat aircraft and carry weapons such as bombs and missiles.

LEFT The American *Global Hawk* UAV first flew in 1998. It can fly for 35 hours without stopping to refuel.

WEAPONS KEY DATES

1400 BC	400 BC	AD 1250	1350	1500
Oldest-known armor worn by soldiers	Wooden crossbow invented	Longbow invented for warfare	Hand cannons first developed	First sailing warships

WARSHIPS

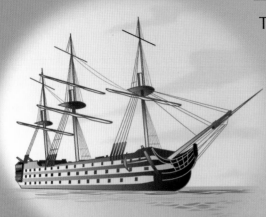

ABOVE *HMS Victory*

When were warships first built?

The first warships were probably built about 3000 BC. They were galleys powered by dozens of oarsmen, but also had sails. By the 1700s, a typical warship, such as the British Admiral Horatio Nelson's famous *HMS Victory*, usually had three tall masts with huge square sails. Known as a "man-of-war," this warship of 1765 was armed with around 100 cannons, fired from three gun decks. After 1860, wooden warships were replaced by armored ships with iron hulls and powered by steam engines.

What were battleships?

Battleships were the largest warships to be developed until aircraft carriers became more important. The largest battleships were over 65,000 tons, over 820 feet long and carried a crew of around 3,000 sailors. They were at the heart of a fleet, accompaniying smaller, faster ships. Their huge guns were designed to bombard coastal targets, or enemy ships as much as 25 miles away.

BELOW A US battleship firing all its guns at once.

DID YOU KNOW?

The first iron battleship, the *Warrior*, was built by the British navy in 1860. The ship's hull was 4½ inches thick to protect it against cannon fire.

LEFT Battleships are heavily armored. They normally work together with other types of warship in groups, called

Why were aircraft carriers invented?

In 1914, the British military created the first aircraft carrier ship to transport planes and fuel across oceans, closer to battle zones. Modern aircraft carriers are enormous floating air bases. They have short runways for fighter jets to take off and land, a control tower for communicating with pilots, and onboard mechanics for servicing the planes.

BELOW Today's aircraft carriers can carry up to 100 aircraft at a time.

How do minesweepers clear mines?

Minesweepers are ships that destroy, neutralize, or remove explosive mines left in the sea by the enemy. Minesweepers may tow along a device that cuts the anchors of moored mines, so they can be removed and made safe. Some tow equipment that gives off signals, like a passing ship, to trigger the mine into exploding without causing any damage. Minesweepers also carry short-range torpedoes designed to blow up mines.

BELOW Minesweepers have hulls made from wood or plastic, since steel hulls would set off magnetic mines in the water.

mine anchored on seabed

A metal wire is towed through the water and cuts the anchor cables of floating mines.

WEAPONS KEY DATES

| 1400 BC Oldest-known armor worn by soldiers | 400 BC Wooden crossbow invented | AD 1250 Longbow invented for warfare | 1350 Hand cannons first developed | 1500 First sailing warships |

SUBMARINES

When was the submarine invented?

The first submarine was built in 1624 for the English King James I. This underwater boat, invented by the Dutchman Cornelius Drebbel had a wooden frame covered with a waterproof skin of greased leather. The submarine was powered by 12 oarsmen, who sat inside the leaking vessel and rowed along under the Thames River. Snorkel airtubes, floating on the surface of the water, enabled the submarine to stay under water for several hours.

RIGHT Submarines are used to seek and destroy ships and other submarines.

What are submarines powered by?

The first modern military submarine was powered by a combination of diesel and electric engines. It was developed by the Irish inventor John P. Holland in 1901. Many submarines still work in the same way today. When traveling on the surface, a diesel engine is used to drive the propeller and push the submarine through the water. An electric motor is used for underwater operations. Since 1954, many submarines have run on nuclear-powered engines. These enable submarines to stay hidden underwater for months at a time without refueling.

DID YOU KNOW?
Small nonmilitary submarines, called submersibles, are used for special underwater tasks, such as exploring shipwrecks or studying ocean life.

A submarine has a stream-lined hull to cut through water easily.

control room

crew's living quarters

The periscope allows the captain to see what is on the surface while the submarine is underwater.

How do submarines work?

Today's submarines have strong steel hulls to withstand high water pressure. A submarine can dive by filling the ballast tanks on either side of its hull with water. This makes the vessel heavier and it sinks. When resurfacing, compressed air is pumped into the tanks to blow the water back out. A submarine has two or three decks divided into many rooms. Sections of the vessel can be closed off in case of leaks in the hull.

Hydroplanes, or fins, tilt for diving and resurfacing.

engine room

LEFT Torpedoes are launched by compressed air from tubes in the nose and rear of the submarine.

propeller

Who invented the torpedo?

The English engineer Robert Whitehead invented the self-propelled torpedo in 1866. These deadly underwater missiles were first used by warships and later carried by military submarines for firing at and sinking enemy ships. Whitehead's weapon had a propeller powered by compressed air to drive it along, and moving fins to steer its path.

The conning tower contains the communication antennas and periscope.

torpedo tube

torpedo room

torpedo tube

LEFT Modern torpedoes have sensors and are guided to their targets by signals from the submarine.

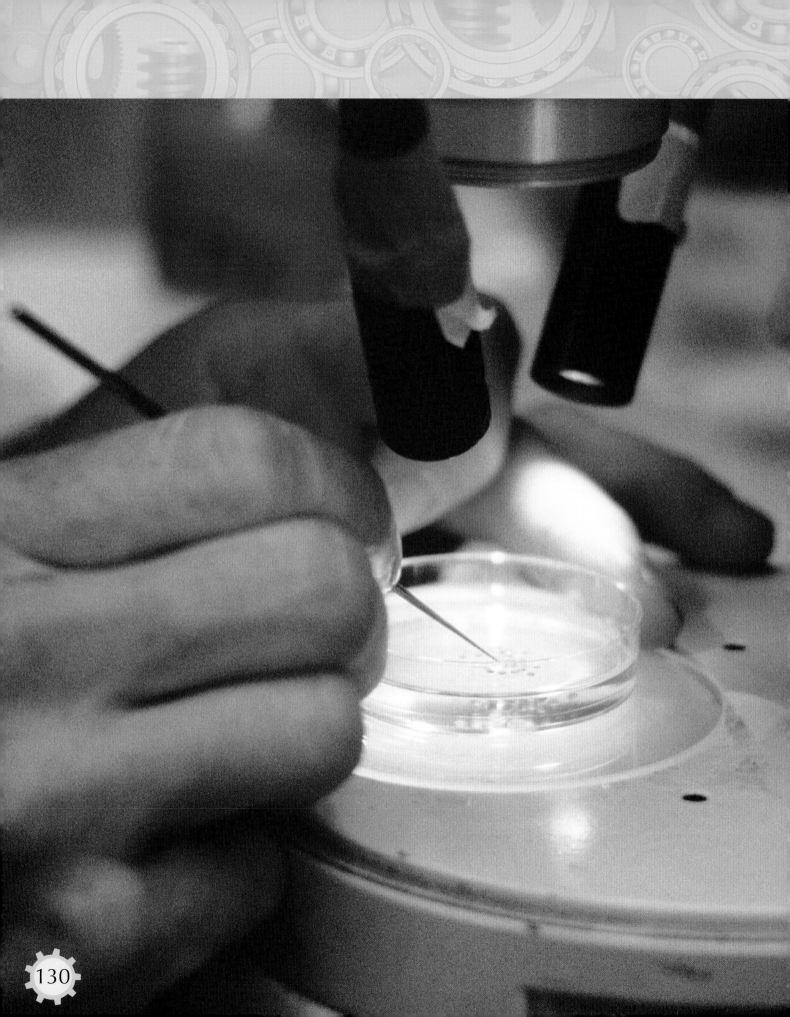

MEDICINE

Discover the role of inventions in improving our health. Learn about microscopes that can magnify a human blood cell hundreds of thousands of times, and how vaccinations that help us fight diseases were invented with the help of a cow! Find out when spectacles were invented and what equipment an ambulance carries to emergencies. Learn about lifesaving machines that can mimic a heartbeat, scanning machines that can make 3-D images of your insides, and surgeons who use miniature cameras to perform operations.

 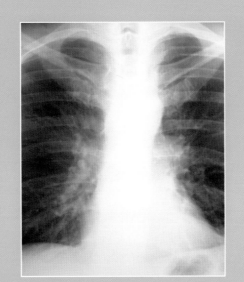 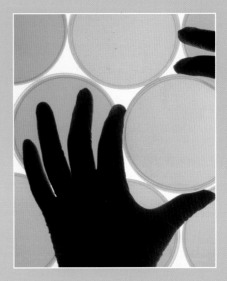

MEDICINE KEY DATES

| AD 1286 | 1592 | 1683 | 1792 | 1796 |
| Spectacles first used as reading glasses | First simple thermometer | Simple microscope invented | Ambulances first used on the battlefield | First vaccination developed |

MEDICAL INSTRUMENTS

Who invented the stethoscope?

The French doctor René Laënnec got the idea for the stethoscope after seeing some children playing with a wooden plank. When a child scratched the plank at one end, another child could hear the scratching sounds by putting an ear to the other end. Laënnec's first stethoscope, made in 1816, was a simple, hollow wooden tube. One end was placed on the patient's chest while the doctor listened at the other end to the patient's heartbeat and breathing.

LEFT Laënnec's first wooden stethoscope

RIGHT Electronic medical thermometers show body temperature on a digital display.

LEFT Modern stethoscopes transmit chest sounds through tubes to the doctor's ears.

When was the thermometer invented?

The Italian scientist Galileo Galilei invented a thermometer to measure temperature in 1592. In 1714, the German physicist Gabriel Fahrenheit invented a precise thermometer using a sealed glass tube containing alcohol. The liquid expanded and rose when heated, and contracted and dropped when cooled. The temperature was shown by the level of the liquid in the tube.

How does a blood-pressure gauge work?

The blood-pressure gauge, first invented in 1863, tests how well a person's heart and blood vessels are working. An inflatable cuff is placed around the patient's arm and pumped up to stop the blood flow. As the pressure in the cuff is released, the blood starts to flow again and a measurement is taken from the attached gauge. A second measurement is then taken when the blood is left to flow naturally.

DID YOU KNOW?
Doctors first started using medical bags during the wars of the late 19th and early 20th centuries. The bags contained all the medical instruments doctors needed to treat wounded soldiers on the battlefield.

hand pump

inflatable cuff

pressure gauge

light beam

magnifying lens

What is an otoscope?

The otoscope is a handheld instrument that doctors use to examine inside a patient's ears. By shining a narrow beam of light into the ear canal and looking through a magnifying lens at the back of the otoscope, a doctor can check the eardrum for signs of infection or disease.

133

MEDICINE KEY DATES

AD 1286	1592	1683	1792	1796
Spectacles first used as reading glasses	First simple thermometer	Simple microscope invented	Ambulances first used on the battlefield	First vaccination developed

MICROSCOPES

DID YOU KNOW?
Optical, or light, microscopes can magnify specimens between 100 to 2,000 times. However, the most powerful electron microscopes can magnify things several million times!

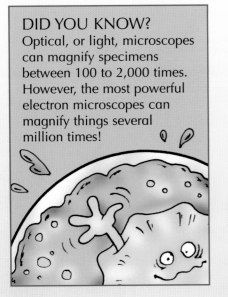

BELOW Scientists today use binocular microscopes to view specimens with both eyes at once.

When was the microscope invented?

The Dutch scientist Anton van Leeuwenhoek invented the first successful simple microscope in 1683. A microscope magnifies tiny objects to show details in close-up that otherwise could not be seen. Leeuwenhoek's microscope had a single, powerful lens that could magnify specimens about 200 times. By putting his eye close to the lens, he could study blood cells and view and sketch microbes, the germs that cause disease.

Screw for focusing

The convex lens was fixed between two metal plates.

Pin for holding the specimen

How does a compound microscope work?

Compound microscopes use two or more lenses to magnify objects up to 2,000 times. The English scientist Robert Hooke improved the design of the early compound microscope in 1660. Compound microscopes have one lens close to the specimen that creates a magnified image inside the barrel. The second lens in the eyepiece then magnifies this image again to give a much bigger total magnification of the object.

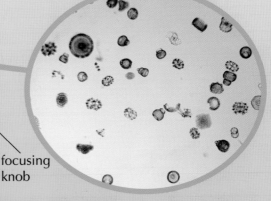

eyepiece lenses

barrel

lens

focusing knob

LEFT Magnified image of microscopic cells on a glass slide. Light shines onto the specimen from below.

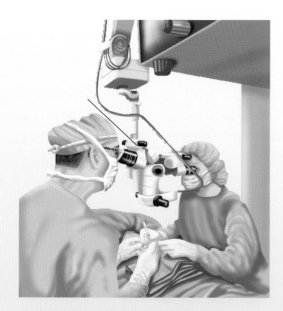

What is microsurgery?

Microsurgery is surgery performed using one or more powerful microscopes. The microscopes enable surgeons to see tiny blood vessels or nerves that have been broken and stitch them back together. One of the first microsurgery operations was performed in the US in 1962. Two doctors worked together to successfully reattach a young boy's right arm, which had been lost in an accident.

LEFT Surgeons use microscopes to view their work in close-up detail.

Who invented the electron microscope?

Ernst Ruska built the first electron microscope in Germany in 1931. His invention magnified specimens using a beam of tiny particles called electrons instead of light. Scanning electron microscopes, developed in the 1960s, are an important research tool for today's doctors and scientists. A scanning electron microscope can magnify minuscule objects, such as blood cells, by hundreds of thousands of times. A beam of electrons is scanned over the surface of a specimen. The reflected electrons form a detailed image on a computer screen for viewing.

Scientists study highly magnified images of specimens on a computer screen.

Specimens, such as these red blood cells, viewed in a beam of electrons appear in shades of gray.

135

MEDICINE KEY DATES

| AD **1286** Spectacles first used as reading glasses | **1592** First simple thermometer | **1683** Simple microscope invented | **1792** Ambulances first used on the battlefield | **1796** First vaccination developed |

VACCINATIONS AND ANTIBIOTICS

When were vaccinations invented?

The English doctor Edward Jenner gave the first vaccination in 1796 against the killer disease smallpox. A vaccination infects the body with a mild form of a disease, which protects people against a more severe attack of the same disease later on. Jenner used germs from the related disease cowpox as his vaccine and called the process vaccination after the Latin word, *vacca,* for cow.

RIGHT Vaccines are injected with a hyperdermic syringe into a patient's bloodstream, which carries it around the body.

How do vaccinations work?

A vaccine contains a weakened form of the bacteria, or germs, of a particular disease. When a vaccine is injected into the body, the immune system produces antibodies that attack and destroy the bacteria. Once vaccinated, people who later catch the disease are better able to fight the infection. The antibodies already present in their system can quickly attack and prevent them from becoming seriously ill.

vaccine germ   antibody

bloodstream

ABOVE A vaccine stimulates the body's immune system to produce antibodies against the germs that cause disease.

136

What are antibiotics?

Antibiotics are medicines that doctors use to treat infections or diseases caused by bacteria—tiny living things, invisible to the naked eye. Antibiotics do not work against diseases caused by viruses, such as the common cold, because viruses are nonliving things. Each type of antibiotic works in a different way to destroy a particular kind of bacterium, without affecting the cells inside the body. For example, one antibiotic is designed to stop bacteria from feeding, so that they die before they can reproduce.

ABOVE Most bacteria are harmless to humans. But some produce poisons, which cause infections or allergic reactions in people.

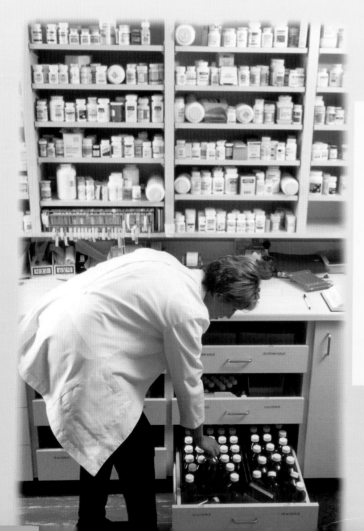

Who discovered the first antibiotic?

In 1928, the Scottish scientist Alexander Fleming discovered that spots of mold growing in one of his laboratory dishes had killed the bacteria he was studying. Other scientists went on to extract penicillin from the mold to create the first antibiotic medicine. Penicillin saved many lives during World War II and has since prevented numerous life-threatening diseases and infections.

LEFT Modern antibiotics are taken in tablet form or as medicine by children. Patients take their doctor's prescription to a pharmacist, who provides them with the right drugs.

MEDICINE KEY DATES

AD 1286	1592	1683	1792	1796
Spectacles first used as reading glasses	First simple thermometer	Simple microscope invented	Ambulances first used on the battlefield	First vaccination developed

SPECTACLES

When were spectacles invented?

Spectacles, or eyeglasses, have not really changed in their basic design since their invention in the 13th century. Italian glassmakers produced the first lenses, which were joined together in a frame for use as reading glasses. People had to balance the spectacles on their nose to help them see more clearly. It wasn't until the 18th century that a frame was designed with arms to support the glasses over the ears.

ABOVE Modern glasses have light plastic lenses to correct the vision of people who are either near- or far-sighted.

LEFT 15th-century spectacles with a bone frame that hinges open to fit on the nose.

beam of light

What is an ophthalmoscope?

The ophthalmoscope is an instrument used by opticians, or eye doctors, to examine the eye. Invented by Hermann von Helmholtz in Germany in 1851, an ophthalmoscope shines a thin beam of light directly into a patient's eye. This enables the optician to see through the pupil to the retina at the back of the eye and check that it is healthy, or work out whether the patient is near- or far-sighted.

Who invented contact lenses?

The first contact lenses to improve eyesight were invented in 1887, by the German scientist Adolf Fick. They were made of heavy, brown glass and could only be worn for a few hours at a time. Since 1938, contact lenses have been made from light plastic. Lenses today are small, curved disks of soft plastic. They are placed directly onto the cornea, over the eye's pupil and iris, and float on the tears that keep the eye moist.

DID YOU KNOW?
The American statesman Benjamin Franklin invented bifocals in 1784. His design combined two lenses—one for close reading, the other for seeing distant objects—in a single frame.

The outer layer of the cornea is lifted back during surgery.

Laser beams flatten or steepen the shape of the cornea so that it works properly again.

ABOVE The first laser eye surgery operations took place in 1995.

How does laser eye surgery work?

Laser eye surgery permanently changes the shape of a person's cornea—the transparent front covering of the eye—to improve the eye's focus. During laser eye surgery, a thin, outer layer of the cornea is treated with alcohol to lift it away from the eye. Then laser rays are beamed at the cornea underneath to reshape it. Once the outer layers are placed back over the cornea, it is able to refract, or focus, light into the eye correctly again.

MEDICINE KEY DATES

| AD 1286 Spectacles first used as reading glasses | 1592 First simple thermometer | 1683 Simple microscope invented | 1792 Ambulances first used on the battlefield | 1796 First vaccination developed |

EMERGENCY VEHICLES

Who invented the ambulance?

The French army surgeon Baron Dominique-Jean Larrey first became famous for the speed with which he could treat wounded soldiers on the battlefield, but he is best remembered as the inventor of the ambulance. During the Napoleonic Wars in 1792, he created a horse-drawn wagon that had room to carry a doctor, nurse, and medical supplies, as well as the injured.

What equipment do ambulances carry?

Modern ambulances carry a wide range of lifesaving equipment and a variety of drugs for medical and accident emergencies. The paramedics on board use oxygen supplies and heart monitors to keep a patient's condition stable during the journey and have a supply of medical dressings for bandaging bleeding wounds. Ambulances are also equipped with flashing warning lights and noisy sirens to warn other drivers to keep out of the way, as they race to reach sick or injured people and transport them quickly to a hospital for treatment.

BELOW All ambulances carry wheeled stretchers for transporting patients.

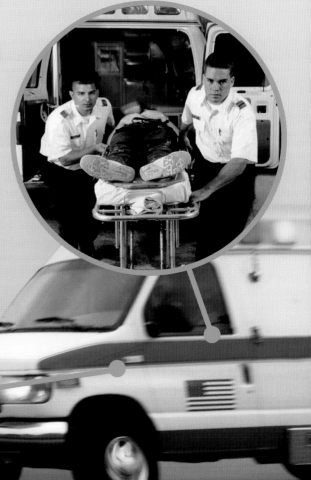

RIGHT Paramedics can give oxygen supplies to a patient suffering breathing difficulties at the site of an emergency.

140

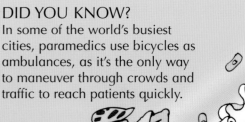

RIGHT Air ambulances are used for medical emergencies in remote places.

DID YOU KNOW?

In some of the world's busiest cities, paramedics use bicycles as ambulances, as it's the only way to maneuver through crowds and traffic to reach patients quickly.

When were air ambulances invented?

Two US army medical officers came up with the idea of moving wounded or sick people by aircraft in 1910, soon after the American Wright brothers successfully flew their first airplane. Captain George H. R. Gosman and Lieutenant A. L. Rhodes built the world's first air ambulance with their own money. Unfortunately, the airplane only flew a short distance before crash-landing on its test flight. Later, in 1928, the world's first successful air ambulance service—now called the Flying Doctors—was set up in the vast Australian outback.

RIGHT Air ambulance helicopters can land their patients directly on top of the hospital roof.

Where do air ambulances operate?

Most air ambulances today are helicopters that operate in and around big cities and can respond within two minutes to an emergency call. These helicopters have special landing gear so that they can put down on all types of terrain. They also have large doors to make it easy to get stretchers in and out. Air ambulances generally carry two pilots, a doctor, and a paramedic and there is space on board for two patients and all the usual lifesaving equipment.

141

MEDICINE KEY DATES

AD 1286	1592	1683	1792	1796
Spectacles first used as reading glasses	First simple thermometer	Simple microscope invented	Ambulances first used on the battlefield	First vaccination developed

LIFESAVING MACHINES

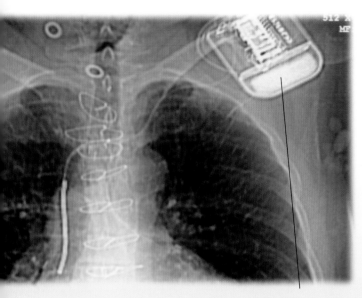

pacemaker implant

Who invented the heart pacemaker?

The Swedish doctors Rune Elmqvist and Åke Senning invented the first heart pacemaker in 1958. They devised a way of implanting a small, battery-operated power source inside the body of patients with a weak heart to give them a strong, regular heartbeat. Pacemakers have extended the lives of thousands of people with heart problems by artificially controlling their heartbeats.

How does a heart pacemaker work?

A pacemaker power unit is implanted under the skin of a patient's body just above the rib cage. Wires, called electrodes, attach this battery-powered electric circuit to the heart. A healthy heart beats in response to natural electrical pulses and pumps blood around the body to keep a person alive. When a weak heart is connected to a pacemaker, it beats each time the electrodes deliver it a small electric shock.

LEFT A pacemaker delivers electrical pulses that make the heart muscles contract and beat regularly.

pacemaker

electrode

heart

142

DOWN The plastic sides of an incubator enclose the baby to keep germs out and warm air in.

When were baby incubators invented?

The first incubators were used in the 1880s to help keep premature babies warm. These babies were born too early and to help them survive, they were placed in wooden cribs, warmed underneath by pans of hot water. Premature babies today spend their early weeks inside an incubator made of transparent plastic. This keeps the newborn babies warm at a steady temperature and safe from infection, as they grow and develop.

DID YOU KNOW?
In 1957, the first-ever artificial heart was implanted inside a dog. The heart was made of plastic and driven by compressed air.

BELOW Patients needing dialysis treatment use a kidney machine about three times a week.

blood tubes

What are kidney machines?

Kidneys are vital organs that filter the blood to remove waste substances and fluid that could be poisonous to the human body. In 1914, scientists invented a kidney, or dialysis, machine that could filter blood outside of the body and save the lives of people with faulty kidneys. When connected to the machine, a patient's blood is pumped through filtering tubes and the cleansed blood is then fed back into the patient's body.

kidney machine

143

MEDICINE KEY DATES

| AD 1286 Spectacles first used as reading glasses | 1592 First simple thermometer | 1683 Simple microscope invented | 1792 Ambulances first used on the battlefield | 1796 First vaccination developed |

X-RAYS AND BODY SCANS

ABOVE This X-ray photograph of a patient's chest shows the skeleton as a light area on a black background.

Who discovered X-rays?

The German physicist Wilhelm Röntgen first discovered X-rays in 1895. X-rays are invisible energy waves, somewhat like light. Röntgen found that X-rays can travel through certain materials and could be used to take photographs inside the human body. Doctors today use X-ray machines to view internal injuries, such as broken bones, or diagnose diseases without using surgery. X-ray beams are directed at the patient's body and pass through softer areas of flesh, but are blocked by harder parts, such as bones and teeth. The X-ray shadows are then captured on photographic film.

BELOW A patient must lie still inside a CAT scan machine, which takes many X-ray pictures of the body.

How do CAT scans work?

Computed Axial Tomography scans, or CAT scans for short, were first developed in the 1960s. A CAT scan machine takes hundreds of X-ray pictures as it scans through a patient's body, slice by slice. These flat, two-dimensional X-ray pictures are then put together on a computer to create a three-dimensional image. Doctors can use the final scan image to examine the inside of a patient's body from many angles.

When were MRI scans invented?

The first Magnetic Resonance Imaging, or MRI, scans were made in the 1970s. An MRI scan can create three-dimensional images of a person's internal organs and display the abnormal cells that cause disease. Inside an MRI scanning machine, the patient is surrounded by a magnetic field and scanned with radio waves, which are absorbed by atoms inside the body. The scanner analyzes these waves to create the MRI images.

RIGHT This MRI scan has been colored to show different parts of a patient's brain.

DID YOU KNOW?
Before doctors realized that too many X-rays can be harmful to health, X-ray machines were commonly used in shoe shops. Clerks took X-rays to see the shape of their customers' feet.

What is an ultrasound scan?

Since the 1960s, ultrasound scanning machines have been used to check on the health of a baby growing inside its mother. High-frequency sound waves —sounds that are too high-pitched for humans to hear—are scanned into a patient's body. Unlike X-rays, ultrasound waves reflect off soft organs and bounce back as echoes, which are displayed as moving images on a monitor screen.

BELOW A probe is moved over the mother's belly and ultrasound waves scan her baby's movements.

145

MEDICINE KEY DATES

AD 1286	1592	1683	1792	1796
Spectacles first used as reading glasses	First simple thermometer	Simple microscope invented	Ambulances first used on the battlefield	First vaccination developed

SURGERY

LEFT Patients undergoing surgery inhaled the ether vapours through a mouthpiece.

When were anesthetics invented?

Before the invention of anesthetics in 1844, patients had to bite down on a stick or get knocked out with alcohol to endure the pain of surgery. The American dentist Horace Wells was the first to use nitrous oxide, commonly called laughing gas, as an anesthetic to dull the pain when pulling out a patient's teeth. A few years later, ether was commonly used as a more effective anesthetic to keep patients unconscious during surgery.

Who first used antiseptics in surgery?

In 1865, the Scottish surgeon Joseph Lister started the practice of spraying carbolic acid, a strong germ killer, around his operating room. Before this time, operating rooms were dangerous places for patients, who very often died from infections caught during surgery. Lister's antiseptic surgery paved the way for modern, safe operating conditions.

DID YOU KNOW?
The first operating rooms were built with standing areas for students to watch the surgeons at work and so they were named 'operating theatres'.

What is keyhole surgery?

Keyhole surgery is a technique where operations are carried out by surgeons without having to make large incisions, or cuts, to open up the body. Instead operations are performed through small holes with thin instruments and surgeons are able to see what they are doing with the help of a tiny video camera placed inside the body. Patients who undergo keyhole surgery generally make a quick recovery because smaller cuts heal faster, are less painful, and leave smaller scars.

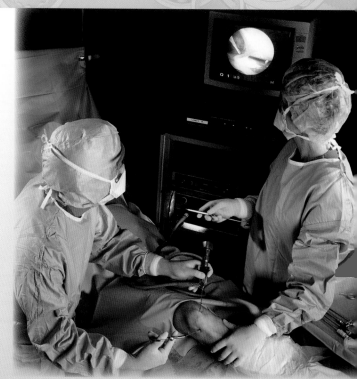

ABOVE Keyhole surgery on a knee

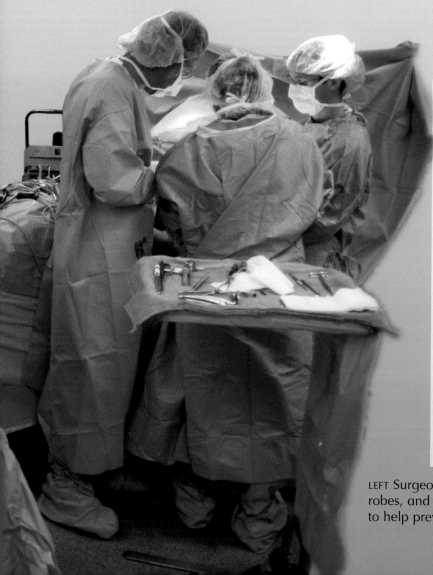

How does keyhole surgery work?

When performing keyhole surgery on a knee, a surgeon inserts a small metal tube into the patient's knee and passes fluid into the area to expand it. Next, a tiny telescope and a miniature video camera are inserted through tubes to project images from inside the knee onto a television screen. The surgeon performs the operation using special surgical instruments inserted through separate holes, while watching his actions on the monitor screen.

LEFT Surgeons today scrub their hands, wear clean robes, and put protective masks over their mouths to help prevent patients from catching infections.

TIME

Measuring time has occupied inventors for centuries.
Early shadow sticks in the ground used the Sun
to show when midday occurred. Today, atomic
clocks are the most accurate timepieces ever made.
Find out how the Egyptians used dripping water to
measure time, and why the first clocks were built
on church towers. Discover why wrist watches
were invented in World War I and how self-winding
watches work. Learn about digital clocks and how
they have become so important in other inventions
we use today, from microwaves to cell phones.

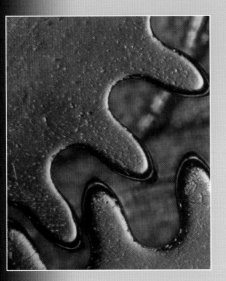

TIME KEY DATES

| 3500 BC | 1400 BC | 1000 BC | AD 1360 | 1510 |
| Shadow sticks used to tell the time | Water clock invented | Sundials used to measure time | First mechanical clock | First portable clock |

SUNDIALS AND EARLY CLOCKS

What is a shadow stick?

An upright stick in the ground casts a shadow that moves as the Sun moves around during the day. The first shadow sticks were used to tell the time as long ago as 3500 BC. People could tell the time of day by looking at the stick's shadow.

BELOW It is thought that the ancient stones of Stonehenge, England, line up with the directions where the Sun and Moon rise and set. They showed the passing of the year like a giant shadow calendar.

BELOW The sundial arm casts a shadow from the Sun.

Who invented the sundial?

The ancient Egyptians invented the sundial to measure time in about 1000 BC. Like shadow sticks, sundials show the time of day using shadows cast by the Sun. Sundials are positioned so that their angled arm is pointing to the North. During the day, the Sun's shadow moves slowly around the dial, which is marked off in hours to indicate the time.

Where were water clocks invented?

Water clocks were invented in Egypt in around 1400 BC. These clocks were more useful than sundials, since they could be used to measure time during the day or night. Water dripped at a steady rate through a hole in one container into a lower one. A scale was marked on the inside of the lower container to show the hours passing as the water level rose. Later, water clocks used the steady drip, or flow, of water to drive around a mechanical wheel that indicated the time.

LEFT Early water clocks used the steady drip of water to measure time.

How is sand used to tell the time?

In a sand clock, the passing of time is measured by sand flowing at a steady rate. The sand empties out of one glass bowl through a narrow gap into another. Many sand clocks are called hourglasses, since they measure a fixed period of one hour. An egg timer is a smaller sand clock that is set to empty in three minutes—the average time needed to boil an egg.

RIGHT Once a sand clock empties, it can be turned over to measure another period of time.

DID YOU KNOW?
King Alfred of England developed the candle clock in around AD 890. Marks made in the wax recorded the passing hours as the candle burned steadily down.

TIME KEY DATES

| 3500 BC Shadow sticks used to tell the time | 1400 BC Water clock invented | 1000 BC Sundials used to measure time | AD 1360 First mechanical clock | 1510 First portable clock |

CLOCKS

Where were the first clocks built?

The first mechanical clocks were built in Europe in around 1360. They replaced water clocks, which could only measure hours. The new clocks were more accurate and later designs chimed every quarter hour, as well as on the hour. The clocks were powered by a falling weight attached to a large cog, or wheel, with teeth. The steady fall of the weight was slowed down by different-sized, interconnecting cogs, which moved the hands around the clock face.

LEFT The first clocks were built in church towers and monasteries so ordinary people knew when to go and pray.

DID YOU KNOW?
The Englishman John Harrison built the first accurate marine clock in 1762. It lost just five seconds in nearly three months at sea. Sailors used Harrison's chronometer to work out the position of the ship on long ocean voyages.

RIGHT Each complete swing of a pendulum takes the same amount of time.

Who invented the pendulum clock?

The Dutch mathematician Christiaan Huygens invented the first working pendulum clock in 1657. His design used the regular, back-and-forth movement of a swinging pendulum to control the clock mechanism. It could measure minutes, as well as quarter hours and hours.

152

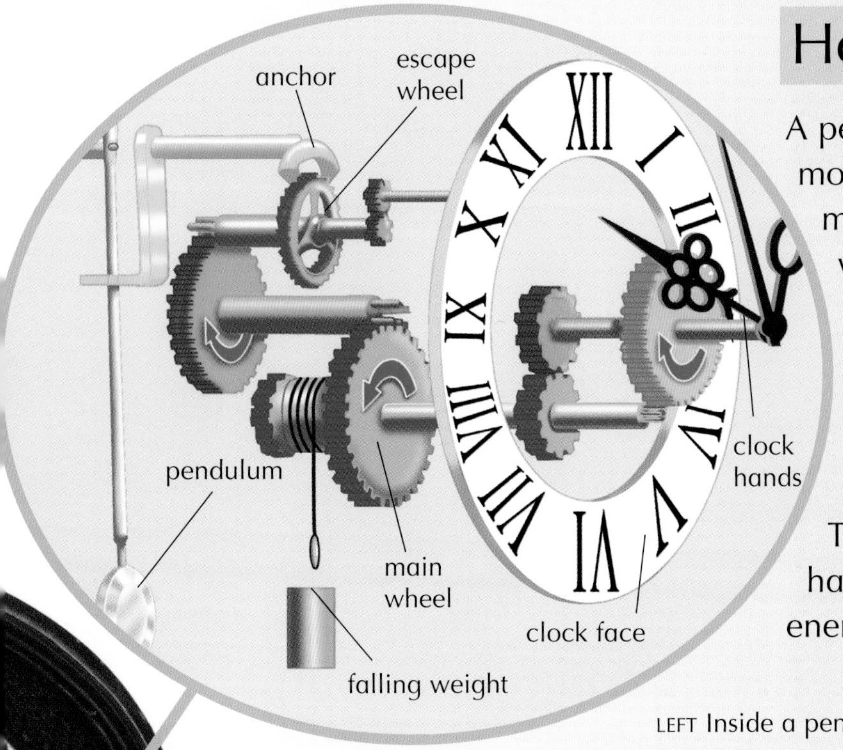

How do pendulum clocks work?

A pendulum clock converts the swinging movement of a pendulum into the turning movement of clock hands. A falling weight drives the clock mechanism. As the pendulum swings left and right, it rocks a lever called the anchor. The regular movement of the anchor releases and grips the escape wheel, allowing it to turn one tooth at a time. The main wheel in turn rotates the clock hands. The falling weight provides the energy to keep all the wheels turning.

anchor

escape wheel

pendulum

main wheel

falling weight

clock hands

clock face

LEFT Inside a pendulum clock

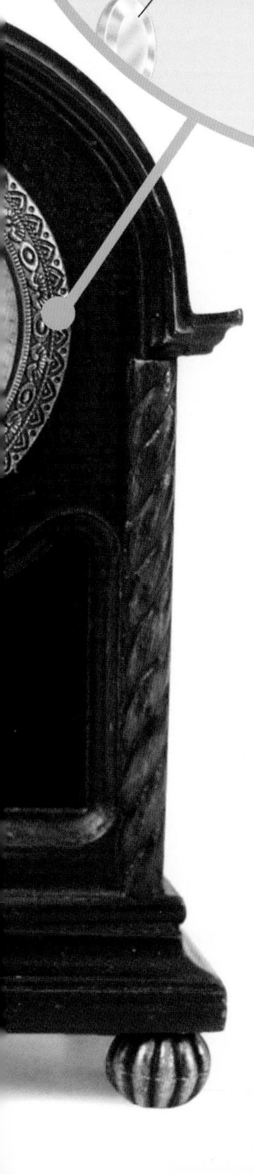

When was the first electric clock?

In 1841, the Scottish clockmaker Alexander Bain invented the first electric clock. It used an electric motor to turn its hands. Up until this time, mechanical clocks had been powered either by using falling weights or by the energy stored in a coiled spring. In the early 1900s, electric clocks became more common because many more people had electricity in their homes.

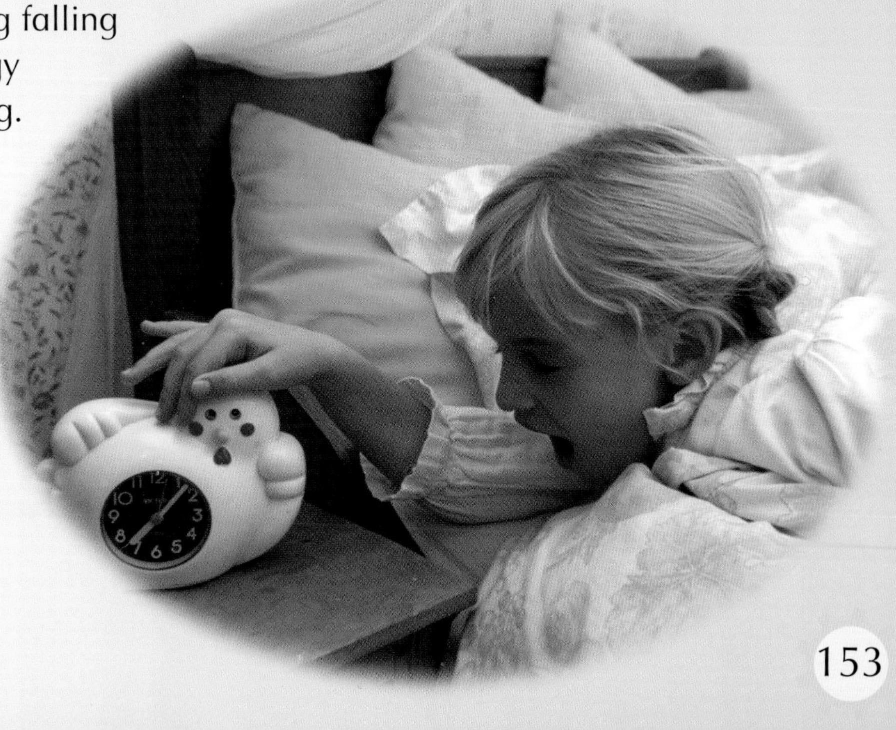

RIGHT This modern alarm clock is battery powered.

153

TIME KEY DATES

| 3500 BC Shadow sticks used to tell the time | 1400 BC Water clock invented | 1000 BC Sundials used to measure time | AD 1360 First mechanical clock | 1510 First portable clock |

WATCHES

BELOW Portable clocks meant that people could carry timepieces around with them for the first time.

When were portable clocks invented?

Peter Henlein, a lockmaker from Germany, invented the first portable mechanical clock in around 1510. It was powered by a coiled spring, which was wound tight using a key. As the mainspring unwound it moved the single hour hand around the clockface. The mainspring took up less space than a falling weight. So the clocks were smaller and lighter, and did not stop working when carried around.

Pocket watches are worn on the end of a short chain.

winder

What powered the first pocket watches?

Early pocket watches were powered by mainsprings. The watch hands moved around at the right speed when the mainspring was wound up tight. But they slowed down as the spring started to unwind. In 1675, Christiaan Huygens invented the hairspring, which kept the watch hands moving at the same speed until the mainspring was wound up again.

DID YOU KNOW?
Modern-style watches first became popular during World War I. They were worn by soldiers in the trenches, where it was easier to glance at a wristwatch than pull out a pocket watch.

BELOW The spring inside a self-winding watch stores enough energy to keep the watch going for about half a day, once removed from the wrist.

rotor

mechanism inside the back of the watch

Modern wristwatches are often waterproof and will work even when wet.

How does a self-winding watch work?

A self-winding watch has a mainspring that is wound up automatically by the movement of the wearer's arm. The mechanism has a semicircular metal weight, called a rotor, which swings back and forth as the watch moves. The rotor is attached to gears that slowly wind up the mainspring, bit by bit. The British watch repairer John Harwood first patented the self-winding wrist watch in 1923.

Who invented the quartz watch?

In 1969, Tsuneya Nakamura and his team of Japanese engineers invented the quartz wristwatch. In a quartz watch, electricity supplied by a battery makes a tiny quartz crystal vibrate at a precise number of pulses per second. These alter the display of a digital watch at the correct rate. In a watch with hands, the pulses control a motor that turns the hands. The regular speed of vibration means that quartz watches are very accurate, only losing or gaining a few seconds each month.

155

TIME KEY DATES

| 3500 BC
Shadow sticks used
to tell the time | 1400 BC
Water clock
invented | 1000 BC
Sundials used to
measure time | AD 1360
First mechanical
clock | 1510
First portable
clock |

DIGITAL CLOCKS

When was the digital clock invented?

The first digital clock was invented in 1968. Digital clocks and watches show time as numbers on an electronic screen, rather than as mechanical hands on a clock face. Early digital displays used small red lights called LEDs, but today's digital clocks use liquid crystal displays or LCDs.

DID YOU KNOW?
Speaking clocks were first introduced in the US in 1927. People could dial a number on the telephone and a machine with a recorded voice told them the correct time.

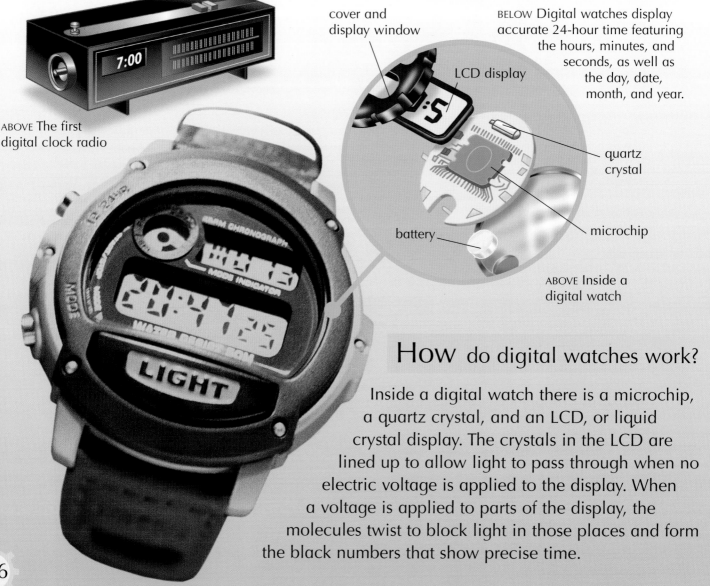

ABOVE The first digital clock radio

cover and display window

LCD display

BELOW Digital watches display accurate 24-hour time featuring the hours, minutes, and seconds, as well as the day, date, month, and year.

quartz crystal

battery

microchip

ABOVE Inside a digital watch

How do digital watches work?

Inside a digital watch there is a microchip, a quartz crystal, and an LCD, or liquid crystal display. The crystals in the LCD are lined up to allow light to pass through when no electric voltage is applied to the display. When a voltage is applied to parts of the display, the molecules twist to block light in those places and form the black numbers that show precise time.

What is an atomic clock?

Atomic clocks are the most accurate of all clocks, since they lose or gain only one second in hundreds of millions of years. These clocks use the regular vibration of atoms to measure time. First invented in 1955, today's atomic clocks give us the precise, standard time that is used by many countries around the world. Modern navigation systems also rely on atomic time signals sent from satellites in space to work out exact locations on Earth.

BELOW Atomic clocks are used by scientists to measure periods of time with amazing accuracy.

BELOW Computer screens often feature a digital clock that displays the day, date, and time. The clock can also be used to flash timed messages on the computer screen to remind the user when tasks need to be done.

Thu 11:15

Where are digital clocks used today?

Today, digital clock displays are found not only on watches, but also on many everyday electronic objects such as cell telephones, radios, DVD players, ovens, cameras, and computers. These clocks not only tell the time, but they can also be programmed to control what the machines do, such as setting a microwave oven to cook food for a specific length of time.

DAILY LIFE

Inventions play a vital part in our homes, even though we may not notice. Find out how a fridge-freezer works, how melting chocolate led to the invention of the microwave oven, and the way early vacuum cleaners were pulled from house to house on a horse-drawn cart. Discover the inventions that have changed the way we shop, from the first coins and paper currency to Internet shopping and smart credit cards that transfer money with a single swipe. Learn why Velcro was inspired by walking the dog and how fleece jackets can be made from old plastic bottles.

DAILY LIFE KEY DATES

400 BC	100 BC	AD 800	1596	1893
Romans build central heating hypocaust	First coins made in China	Chinese invent paper money	Flushing toilet invented	Zipper invented to replace bootlaces

KEEPING CLEAN

ABOVE The Romans piped hot water from thermal springs underground.

When were baths invented?

The first record of bathtubs is in Babylonia over 4,500 years ago. They were filled with river water fetched by slaves. Today, the water that fills your bath begins its journey at a reservoir where rainwater is stored. It is then filtered and cleaned before traveling through underground pipes to our homes. Here it is heated by a water heater that pumps it through pipes into the faucet.

Who invented the toilet?

The first flushing toilet was invented in 1596 by the Englishman Sir John Harrington. At first, only the very wealthy could afford a private lavatory. Most people used chamber pots at night and threw their waste into open sewers in the street in the morning. When millions of people in Europe died from cholera in 1832, laws were passed encouraging everyone to use toilets.

RIGHT The flush handle opens a valve to let water from the tank fill the toilet bowl.

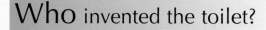

LEFT Early lavatories were often highly decorated because they were prized possessions.

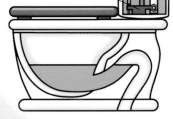

float
flush handle
overflow pipe
flush valve

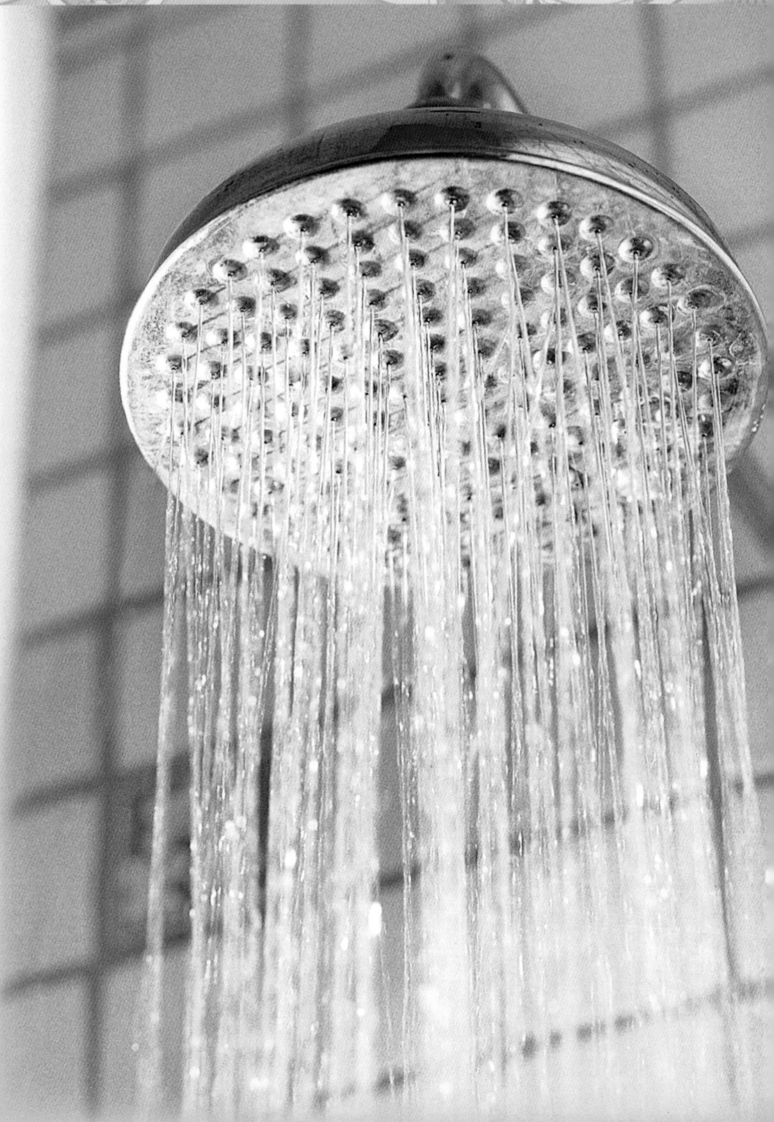

What were the first showers?

The first showers were probably invented when people realized they could get clean by standing under the fast-flowing water from waterfalls. Then people started pouring water over themselves from buckets. One of the earliest showers to be built inside a house was 10 feet high and was developed in 1810 for the bathroom of a grand English manor house.

DID YOU KNOW?
In ancient Greece, people invented dentures (false teeth) from fake and real teeth held together with pieces of gold wire!

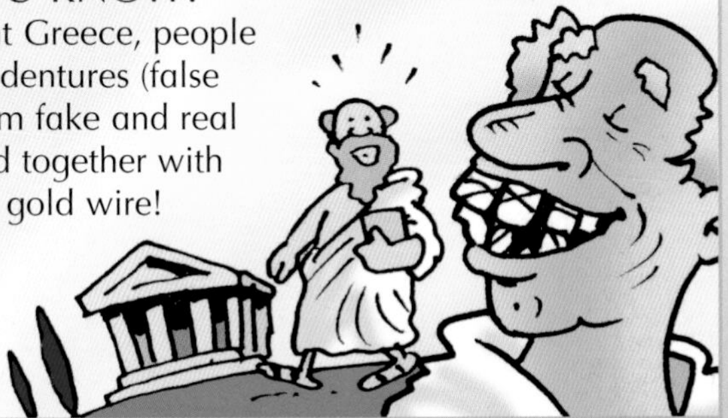

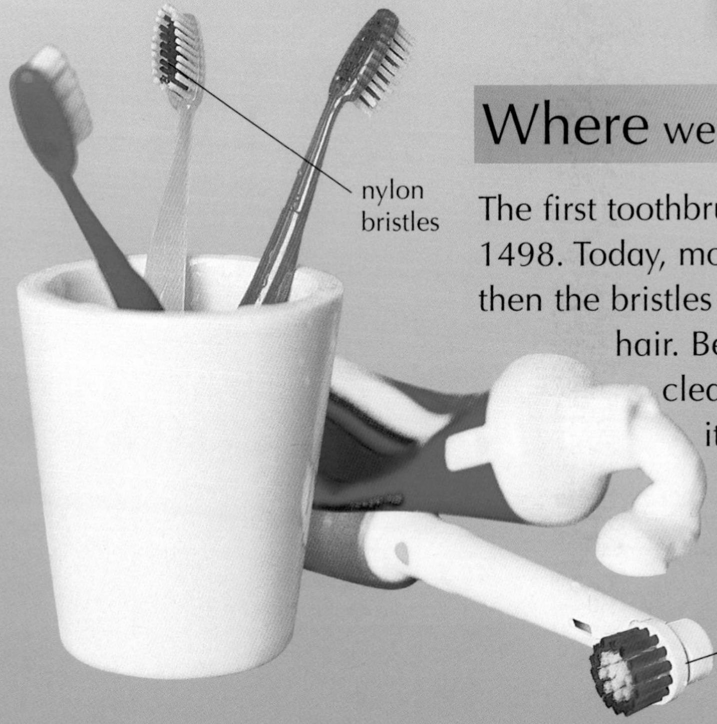

nylon bristles

Where were toothbrushes invented?

The first toothbrush with bristles was invented in China in 1498. Today, most toothbrushes have nylon bristles, but then the bristles were made from pig-, horse-, or badger-hair. Before the toothbrush was invented, people cleaned their teeth with a stick mashed until it was soft and shredded. The first electric toothbrushes were invented around 1978.

Electric toothbrushes have heads driven by a motor that do a lot of the brushing work for you.

161

DAILY LIFE KEY DATES

| **400 BC** Romans build central heating hypocaust | **100 BC** First coins made in China | **AD 800** Chinese invent paper money | **1596** Flushing toilet invented | **1893** Zipper invented to replace bootlaces |

HEATING

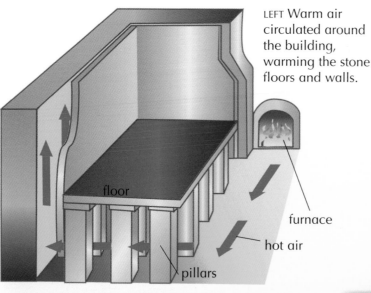

LEFT Warm air circulated around the building, warming the stone floors and walls.

floor

furnace

hot air

pillars

Who invented central heating?

Keeping homes warm has always been a challenge in cold places or during winter. The ancient Romans invented the first central heating system, called a hypocaust, in 400 BC. A fire in a room against an outside wall fed heated air under the house. The floors were raised on pillars and the walls were hollow so the heat flowed around the whole building warming the stone walls and floors.

Where were gas fires invented?

The first really successful gas fires for the home were invented in England by engineer Sigismund Leoni in 1881. A gas valve or tap is turned to release gas from a pipe and the gas is lit. Heat comes from the gently burning gas, but many fires also have fake coals or rocks that glow red hot.

DID YOU KNOW?
In Iceland, water heated by hot rocks underground comes to the surface in springs. This is collected and piped to homes for heating and for hot tap water!

162

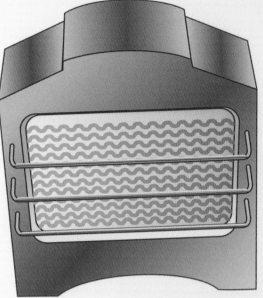

ABOVE An electric current passing through a coiled filament heats it up, warming the air around it.

When was the electric heater invented?

The method for making an electric heater came from several sources, but the first household electric heater was patented in 1892 by Bell Crompton and his partner, Herbert Dowsing in the UK. In an electric heater, electricity passes thro,ugh a heating element. The heating element converts electrical energy into heat energy and as it gets hotter and hotter, some of this heat escapes into the air and warms up the room.

How do radiators work?

In modern central heating systems hot water is pumped through metal radiators. Heat from the radiator warms the air that flows past it. This warm air rises and colder air flows in to take its place. This circulation develops a flow of air around the room, sending warm air away from the radiator and delivering cooler air back to be heated.

RIGHT This type of convection radiator was invented by Franz SanGalli in 1855.

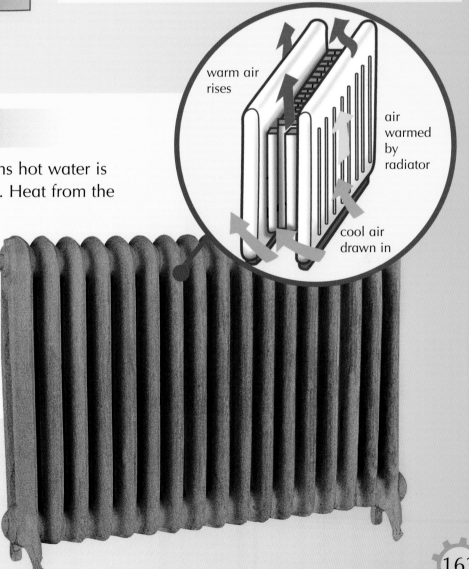

warm air rises

air warmed by radiator

cool air drawn in

163

DAILY LIFE KEY DATES

400 BC	100 BC	AD 800	1596	1893
Romans build central heating hypocaust	First coins made in China	Chinese invent paper money	Flushing toilet invented	Zipper invented to replace bootlaces

WASHING MACHINES

Where was the washing machine invented?

The very first washing machine was made in the US in 1874. It was a wooden tub with small wooden pegs inside that you turned with a handle. Soapy clothes were tumbled around to clean them. The first electric washing machine with a rotating drum was invented in 1907 by Alva J. Fisher in the US. By the 1960s, fully automatic washing machines were available that could wash, rinse ,and spin at the touch of a button.

Wet clothes were lifted out and fed through the wringer to squeeze out the water.

Wooden pegs inside the tub rotated the laundry.

BELOW The washtub was filled by hand with hot soapy water.

BELOW Laundry goes into a drum at the front with a watertight seal around the door.

How does a washing machine work?

Most washing machines work by tumbling dirty laundry, soap, and water around inside a moving drum to loosen the dirt. Then the drum spins round very fast so that the soapy water comes out of the laundry, drains through the little holes in the drum, and flows away. You just have to press a button to program the washing machine's computer to tell it how strong or long each wash needs be.

soap drawer

Draining holes allow water to flow in and out.

spinning drum

Heavy weight to keep the machine in place while it is spinning.

164

1901
Horse-drawn vaccuum cleaner in service

1945
Microwave ovens on sale for first time

1970
First bar code used on chewing gum

1982
Smart card invented for public telephone calls

When was the first dishwasher invented?

The first dishwashers, which appeared in the US around 1900, were turned by hand. Unfortunately, these took a long time to wash a few dishes, leaked a lot, and often didn't work properly. Americans had to wait until the 1940s for the first boxed-in electric dishwasher that also rinsed dishes. They were not available in Europe until 1960.

DID YOU KNOW?
Early washing machines helped clean clothes but washing was made easier still in 1861 when the wringer was invented to get the water out of laundry after washing.

RIGHT Dishwashers clean by spraying hot water and detergent onto dirty dishes. Then clean water rinses away the soapy water.

Why was soap invented?

Water has surface tension and doesn't wash things well, so people invented soap. People began to make soap from about 2800 BC. The soap was made by boiling fat with wood ash, and used to wash clothes. The first artificial laundry soaps, called detergents, were invented in the 1920s, when American chemists created chemicals that loosen dirt from laundry in water, so that the dirt is washed away.

165

DAILY LIFE KEY DATES

400 BC	100 BC	AD 800	1596	1893
Romans build central heating hypocaust	First coins made in China	Chinese invent paper money	Flushing toilet invented	Zipper invented to replace bootlaces

STOVES AND REFRIGERATORS

gas burner

gas tap

gas oven

ABOVE The first gas stoves were made from heavy cast iron.

Who invented the first cooker?

The first gas stove was invented by James Sharp in England in 1826. The first electric stove was invented in the US by William Hadaway in 1896. Gas stoves use flames to heat pans of food, while electric stovetops have a coil of wires that heat up when high-current electricity flows through them.

stirrer magnetron

microwaves

timer

BELOW In a microwave oven, a magnetron tube converts electric current into microwave energy. A "stirrer" rotates to make sure the microwaves don't concentrate in one place.

Who invented the microwave oven?

American researcher Percy Spencer discovered microwaves when he paused in front of some radar equipment and realized the chocolate in his pocket was melting! The chocolate was being cooked by invisible electromagnetic waves called microwaves. The company he worked for sold the first microwave oven in 1945. When something is hot, it's because its molecules are vibrating quickly. Microwaves make water molecules in food vibrate quickly and this cooks the food.

When was the refrigerator invented?

The first refrigerators were invented in England in the 19th century. These were simple wooden boxes lined with metal and an insulating material, such as cork, which held blocks of ice to keep food cool. The first fridges as we know them appeared in 1914. By the 1920s, the first electric refrigerators with freezer compartments were being sold.

DID YOU KNOW?
For hundreds of years people cooked over open fires, but in 1490 the first oven - a brick box that trapped heat from a fire - was invented in France.

ABOVE Refrigerators work by removing heat from inside the appliance.

How do fridge-freezers work?

Refrigerators and freezers work using a special substance called a coolant. The coolant, in the form of a gas, goes through a compressor, where it turns into a liquid. Compressing the coolant makes it warm. The warm liquid passes through zigzag pipes on the outside of the fridge and cools down to room temperature. The coolant is forced through a valve under pressure and expands suddenly, turning into gas and cooling. The cold gas circulates in pipes inside the fridge-freezer, cooling the air and so keeping the food and drinks cool. The gas gets warmer and passes through the compressor to start the cycle again.

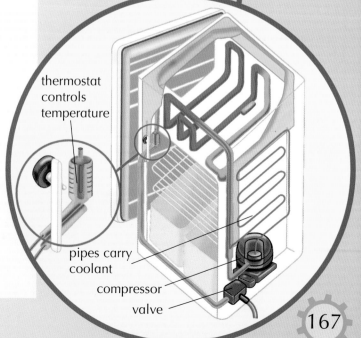

thermostat controls temperature

pipes carry coolant

compressor

valve

167

DAILY LIFE KEY DATES

| **400 BC**
Romans build central
heating hypocaust | **100 BC**
First coins made in
China | **AD 800**
Chinese invent
paper money | **1596**
Flushing toilet
invented | **1893**
Zipper invented to
replace bootlaces |

HOUSEHOLD GADGETS

BELOW The first irons got their name because they were made of the metal iron. They were heated directly over a gas flame or hot oven plate.

Who introduced the electric iron?

American Henry W. Seely introduced the electric iron in 1882 and it was one of the first gadgets made to use electricity. The hot plate of an iron is warmed by a heating element inside. The heat is controlled by a thermostat that switches the electric current on and off to keep it at the right temperature.

DID YOU KNOW?
The first pop-up toaster was invented in the US in 1930s, but the country's economy was in the Depression so few people could afford the luxury of buying one!

When were vacuum cleaners invited?

In 1901, English engineer Cecil Booth came up with the idea of a device to remove dust using suction. He tested the idea by sucking in a handkerchief over a dusty chair and saw that the dust collected on the handkerchief. He patented the first vacuum cleaner, the Puffing Billy, later that year, using a gasoline-burning internal-combustion engine to power the suction. It was so big it had to be pulled from house to house by a horse-drawn cart.

BELOW Today's vaccuum cleaners have small electrical motor. This turns a fan inside, pulling air and dirt in through a filter that collects the dirt in a bag or chamber that can be emptied.

How do hairdryers work?

The first handheld hairdryers were invented in 1920 in the US and, although the outer designs have changed, the insides basically work in the same way today. Hairdryers have metal wires inside that get hot when electricity flows through them. The hot wires heat air as it is blown past them and out through the hairdryer nozzle by a motor-operated fan. The warm air dries your hair by evaporating the water away.

fan
heated filaments
electric motor
nozzle.
switch

Where were food processors invented?

The first food processor was invented in France in 1971 and it was called a Magimix. Food processors save cooks time and energy because they can mix dough and chop, slice, dice, and even liquidize different foods. To make them work, food processors have motors inside that convert electrical energy into spinning movement energy to turn blades and other tools around inside a bowl.

ABOVE The internal workings of a hand-held food mixer

169

DAILY LIFE KEY DATES

400 BC	100 BC	AD 800	1596	1893
Romans build central heating hypocaust	First coins made in China	Chinese invent paper money	Flushing toilet invented	Zipper invented to replace bootlaces

MONEY

ABOVE Early Chinese coins came in many different shapes.

When were coins invented?

The first coins were made in China in 100 BC from roughly shaped metal. Elsewhere in the world, the first coins were made from lumps of silver. Before coins were invented, people swapped goods, or used things like sharks' teeth, cowrie shells, feathers, salt, or even squirrel furs to pay for goods. By 650 BC silver coins of different sizes and weight were made in Turkey, which were weighed and marked with their value.

How are coins made today?

Today, machines make coins out of cheap, lightweight metals. Giant rolls of metal sheet are fed into powerful machines that punch or cut out small, blank disks. Other machines stamp or press the value of the coin onto both sides of the disks, along with words and pictures that show where the coin comes from.

BELOW Coins are made in a factory called a mint.

BELOW New coins are weighed on electronic scales into amounts of currency.

1 Sheets of metal are fed through a blanking machine that presses out disks of the right size.

2 The disks are cleaned and softened by heating, cooling, and washing.

3 A coining machine presses the design of the coin onto each disk. It can make as many as 700 coins each minute!

1901
Horse-drawn vaccuum cleaner in service

1945
Microwave ovens on sale for first time

1970
First bar code used on chewing gum

1982
Smart card invented for public telephone calls

ABOVE US dollar bills are also known as Greenbacks.

Where was paper money invented?

Gold and silver coins were heavy to carry. In AD 800, the Chinese invented a lighter form of money—paper currency. The Romans also used paper money from about AD 1000, but paper money was slow to spread to the rest of the world. By the 1400s, people in parts of India and Japan were using paper money, but the Europeans carried heavy coins until the 1660s.

What are smart cards?

Today, we pay for most things by card—by debit, credit, and, more recently, smart card. Smart cards are credit cards that contain a computer chip. The computer chip stores information, such as how much money you have in your bank account. Smart cards were invented in 1982 for use in telephone booths, but are now used to pay for many different things. When you buy something with a smart card, the chip reduces the amount you have left to spend.

DID YOU KNOW?
Credit cards were invented in 1951 after American Frank McNamara forgot his wallet. His Diners Club card was the first to allow people to have lunch and pay for it later.

computer chip

BELOW Credit and debit cards contain coded information that connects directly with your bank account.

171

DAILY LIFE KEY DATES

| **400** BC | **100** BC | **AD 800** | **1596** | **1893** |
| Romans build central heating hypocaust | First coins made in China | Chinese invent paper money | Flushing toilet invented | Zipper invented to replace bootlaces |

SHOPPING

BELOW Harrods, one of the world's most famous department stores, is lit up for Christmas.

When were shops invented?

The first shops were invented in 650 BC in Turkey, in the same area that silver coins were first used. These were permanent places where goods were bought and sold. Before that, people traded from temporary market stalls. In the 1700s, stores with separate departments that sold different goods first appeared. These were the first department stores.

DID YOU KNOW?
The first self-service supermarkets with parking lots appeared in the US in the 1930s.

RIGHT James Ritty's first cash register.

Who invented the cash register?

The first mechanical cash register was invented in 1879 by an American named James Ritty to keep his staff from stealing change. By pressing keys, the machine added up how much money was spent and showed it on a dial that he could see. Today, most cash registers scan bar codes and people no longer have to punch in numbers.

How do bar codes work?

Bar codes are striped black and white labels that save time at checkouts. A laser on a bar code reader shines a beam of light that bounces off the bar code. The cash register then automatically identifies what the item is and adds its price to your bill. The first product to have a bar code was a packet of Wrigley's Gum in the 1970s.

ABOVE The bar code reader recognizes the unique pattern of stripes on each item in the store.

BELOW Online shopping is quick and easy.

What is Internet shopping?

Shopping on the Internet is just like ordering something over the telephone, except you use a computer to do it. You usually pay for an item by credit card and stores deliver the goods to your home. The first Internet shopping site was Amazon.com, which began selling books in 1995. American computer scientist Jeff Bezos is said to have started the business from his garage.

DAILY LIFE KEY DATES

400 BC	100 BC	AD 800	1596	1893
Romans build central heating hypocaust	First coins made in China	Chinese invent paper money	Flushing toilet invented	Zipper invented to replace bootlaces

CLOTHING

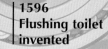

RIGHT Zippers that open at the bottom were not invented until the 1960s.

Who invented the zipper?

In 1893, American engineer Whitcomb Judson got fed up with tieing his boots and wanted a quicker way to fasten them. He invented the "clasp-locker"—a series of hooks and eyes. The first modern-style zipper was designed in 1913 and patented in 1917 by Gideon Sundback. The zipper got its name from the zipper boot. A zipper has lots of metal or plastic teeth with ridged edges that join together when the slider is pulled in one direction and undo when the slider is pulled in the other direction.

clasp

teeth

Where was waterproof cloth invented?

Waterproof cloth was invented in Glasgow, Scotland, a famously rainy city, in 1823. Its creator combined rubber and fabric to make waterproof cloth for raincoats. The inventor was Charles Macintosh, which is why raincoats are called Mackintoshes or Macs in the UK. Some modern raincoats are still made from rubber and plastic. Most are made from plastic-coated artificial fibres. Some fabrics can be coated with a durable water repellant. This makes the water stay in small droplets and drip off the fabric, instead of soaking in.

ABOVE Spandex is lightweight, stretchable and strong.

When were artificial fabrics invented?

The first artificial fabric, nylon, was invented in 1938 in the US, but it was created by scientists from both New York and London, and that is how it got its name NY-Lon. In 1959, Spandex was invented by Joseph Shivers in the US. Like nylon and Spandex, many new fabrics, such as polyester and acrylic, are woven from plastic fibers made from oil.

BELOW It takes about 25 two-liter soda bottles to make a fleece jacket from recycled plastic.

How are fleece jackets made?

Many fleece jackets are made from polyester, but oil is a limited resource and some fleece jackets are being made from recycled plastic bottles instead. The used bottles are chopped up into flakes, cleaned, dried, and melted. The melted plastic is made into long strands of fiber, which are spun into yarn, woven into fabric, then cut and sewn into a jacket.

DID YOU KNOW?
In 1907 George De Mestral got the idea for Velcro from his dog! He noticed that burrs (seed sacs) stuck to fur with tiny hooks. Velcro fasteners have tiny hooks on one side that attach to tiny loops on another.

COMMUNICATIONS

The way we pass information to each other is an important aspect of our daily lives and many clever inventions help us communicate. Discover what the first paper was made from, how feathers were used as pens, and when the first books were printed. Learn what the first words ever to be spoken over a telephone were, and how radios can carry voices around the globe. Find out how computers have shrunk from the size of a room to fit on a lap, how email works, and what the www. really means.

COMMUNICATIONS KEY DATES

| AD 150 | AD 500 | 1450 | 1660 | 1844 |
| Paper first invented | Quill pens used with ink | First printing press | First postal service introduced | Electric telegraph in use |

PAPER AND PENS

When was paper invented?

The first kind of paper, called papyrus, was invented in 3000 BC by the ancient Egyptians. They hammered together the stems of a reedlike plant, called sedge, to form sheets. Once dry, the papyrus sheets could be rolled up into scrolls. Paper, as we know it today, was invented in China in about AD 150. The Chinese court official Tsai Lun found that grinding up woody plants and soaking their fibers in water produced a pulp. This could then be pressed and dried into sheets of paper.

ABOVE Until paper-making reached Europe, vellum made from animal skin was used for manuscripts and books.

ABOVE The Chinese art of papermaking didn't reach Europe until a thousand years after its invention, in around AD 1150.

What did people first write with?

Ancient Egyptian writers, called scribes, used hollow reeds and ink to write on papyrus in around 3000 BC. In AD 150, Chinese writers became skilled in the art of calligraphy. They produced fine lettering using ink and brushes made of bamboo stems and tufts of hair. From around AD 500 until 1830, writers used quill pens made out of long goose feathers. The feather tip, or nib, was sharpened to a point with a penknife. Then it was dipped in ink for writing. From the 1880s, people used fountain pens with steel writing nibs and an in-built supply of ink.

RIGHT The hollow center of the quill pen held enough ink for a sentence of writing.

Who invented the ballpoint pen?

In 1938, two Hungarian brothers living in Argentina designed the first successful ballpoint pen. The journalist Ladislao Biro together with his brother Georg, a chemist, developed a pen that used quick-drying ink. It had a small, metal rolling ball in the writing tip. Their ballpoint pen is sometimes called the "biro" and since the mid 1940s, it has been widely used around the world.

LEFT As you write, the metal ball in a ballpoint pen turns in its socket. The ball rolls ink from inside the ink cartridge onto the paper.

BELOW Information can be written directly onto a touch-screen with a stylus. The words and numbers are then stored in the PDA's memory.

DID YOU KNOW?
In 2005, scientists discovered a way of making a waterproof coating for paper. The paper can be written on with pencil or ink, but doesn't fall apart when wet.

Which pens can write on screens?

With a special pen, called a stylus, you can write words directly onto the touch-screen of an electronic personal organizer. Personal digital assistants, or PDAs for short, are handheld, minicomputers that people use for keeping addresses, taking notes, and recording information. Using the stylus you can enter text by tapping letters displayed on the touch-screen keyboard. The first touch-screen PDAs were produced in the US in 1996.

179

COMMUNICATIONS KEY DATES

AD 150	AD 500	1450	1660	1844
Paper first invented	Quill pens used with ink	First printing press	First postal service introduced	Electric telegraph in use

PRINTING

Why was the printing press invented?

The earliest books were rare and expensive because they were written out by hand. The invention of the printing press meant many copies of a book could be printed quickly, so that more people could read it. The German goldsmith Johann Gutenberg perfected the first printing press in 1450. He made raised metal letters on blocks, called type. These were arranged as words in lines to form each page. Black ink was rolled onto the type and the letters were pressed onto paper to copy each page.

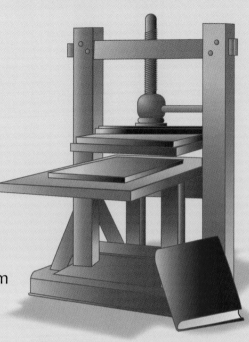

ABOVE It took two or three people to produce one page using Gutenberg's printing press.

DID YOU KNOW?
The earliest books were printed in China in around AD 868. Words and pictures were carved into wooden blocks. These were then inked and pressed onto paper.

BELOW A typewriter from the early 1900s

ink ribbon

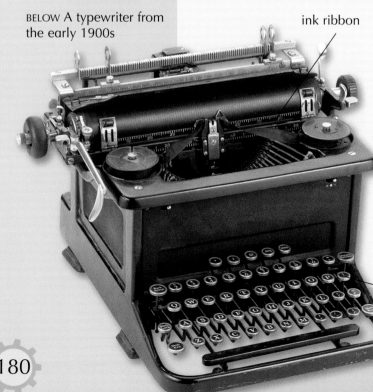

Who invented the typewriter?

The first successful typewriter, invented by the American Christopher Sholes, was put on sale in 1874. His writing machine enabled fast typists to make neat printed pages of text without jamming the keys. The design slowed typists down slightly by placing the common letter keys in positions that are harder to hit.

The QUERTYUIOP arrangement of letter keys designed by Sholes is still used on computer keyboards today.

How are pages printed today?

Today, the color pages of books and magazines are usually printed on offset printing presses. Computer software is used to convert designed pages into flat metal printing plates. There are separate plates for four basic colored inks—cyan, magenta, yellow and black—and each one is wrapped around a cylinder. One ink color is rolled onto the plate as the cylinder rotates. Water is also rolled onto the plate to keep the non-printing areas ink-free. The plate then transfers the inked page onto a soft, rubber roller, which prints the words and pictures onto a roll of paper. Once the paper dries, it is overprinted in the same way with the inks on the other three color plates.

water rollers

ink rollers

impression cylinder

plate cylinder

offset rubber cylinder

paper

ABOVE Automated, offset printing presses are very fast and accurate.

What is desktop publishing?

Desktop publishing started in 1985, when people were first able to use page design software on their personal computers. They could create their own documents and print them inexpensively on a laser printer. Desktop publishing software enables anyone to design pages with different styles of type and headings and include pictures such as photographs and graphics. Once the laser printer receives the image data from the computer, it can quickly and quietly print multiple copies of the finished color pages.

ABOVE Laser printers are widely used to print personal documents.

COMMUNICATIONS KEY DATES

AD 150	AD 500	1450	1660	1844
Paper first	Quill pens used	First printing	First postal service	Electric telegraph
invented	with ink	press	introduced	in use

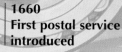

TELEPHONES

What was the electric telegraph?

The electric telegraph was first used in 1844 to send a message between the American cities of Washington and Baltimore. This communications system transmitted the letters of the alphabet using a code of dots and dashes. It was invented by the Americans, Samuel Morse, Joseph Henry, and Alfred Vail. A "Morse code" message was sent down a cable from one telegraph station to another by tapping a key. This switched the electric power supply on and off. A receiver at the other end recorded the signals as dots and dashes. The code was then translated back into words.

DID YOU KNOW?
Videophones were first made in the 1990s to let callers see the person they were talking to. A small video camera records the caller's face. The pictures are sent down the phone line to the videophone's TV screen.

RIGHT A telegraph key was used to tap out Morse code messages.

BELOW Early telephones had no dials or keys for putting in phone numbers. All calls were connected by an operator.

microphone for speaking

earphone for listening

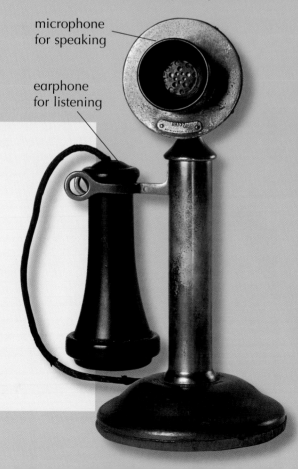

Who invented the telephone?

In 1875, the Scottish inventor Alexander Graham Bell became the first person to transmit the human voice along an electrical wire. Bell had been looking for a way of sending several telegraph messages at once down a wire, when he accidently spilled acid on his clothes. As Bell cried for help, his assistant heard his words, "Mr. Watson! Come here, I want you!" coming from the machine they had built. This surprise discovery led to his invention of the telephone in 1876.

1876
First telephone
invented

1896
First radio
transmitter

1938
Ballpoint pen
developed

1977
First personal
computer

1981
Internet opened
to the public

BELOW The telephone network

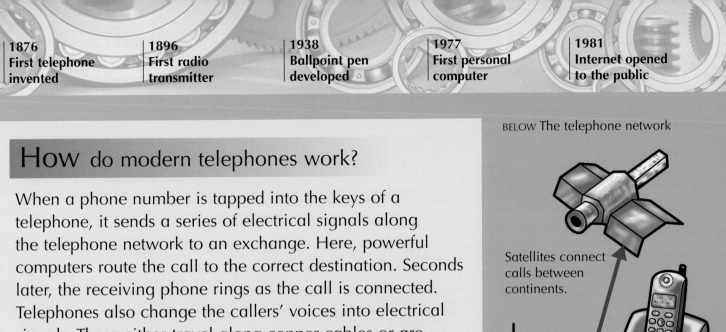

How do modern telephones work?

When a phone number is tapped into the keys of a telephone, it sends a series of electrical signals along the telephone network to an exchange. Here, powerful computers route the call to the correct destination. Seconds later, the receiving phone rings as the call is connected. Telephones also change the callers' voices into electrical signals. These either travel along copper cables or are changed into pulses of light and sent along optical fibers made of thin strands of glass. International calls are sent via satellite links, which transmit the signals as radio waves.

Satellites connect calls between continents.

The caller's phone dials a number.

The local exchange connects local numbers or routes the call to a national exchange.

The receiver's phone rings when the call is connected.

The national exchange forwards the call.

The cell phone exchange connects calls to cell phones.

When were cell phones invented?

The first cell, or mobile, phone was developed in 1973 by the American Martin Cooper. Early mobile phones were known as car phones, since they were designed for use in a car. Today's cell phones allow people to make and receive calls from almost anywhere. They work by sending and receiving calls using invisible radio-wave signals. These travel through the air to a nearby mobile phone exchange, which connects the call through to the right number.

RIGHT Your cell phone information is stored on a SIM card (Subscriber Identity Module)

183

COMMUNICATIONS KEY DATES

AD 150	AD 500	1450	1660	1844
Paper first invented	Quill pens used with ink	First printing press	First postal service introduced	Electric telegraph in use

RADIO

Who invented radio?

The Italian electrical engineer Guglielmo Marconi combined the ideas of other inventors to build the first successful radio transmitter in 1896. It used electric sparks to create radio waves that were picked up by a receiver over four miles away. Radio transmitters work by turning sound into electrical signals, which are in turn changed into radio waves. Invisible radio waves can travel long distances through the air at the speed of light.

BELOW Marconi's radio transmitter

What was the first radio broadcast?

The earliest radio transmissions were messages sent in Morse code, often for the military. In 1906, the first sound radio broadcast was made in the US by the Canadian inventor, Reginald Fessenden. He used his transmitter to broadcast music and a reading from the Bible to the public. However, Fessenden's audience was small, since home radio receivers were not available for sale until the 1920s.

BELOW Early radio receivers, like this one, were called a "wireless" because they picked up signals without needing telegraph cables.

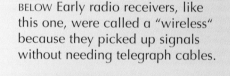

DID YOU KNOW?
The British inventor Trevor Baylis built the world's first successful clockwork radio in 1991. The radio is powered by winding a handle, which charges the batteries inside.

1876
First telephone invented

1896
First radio transmitter

1938
Ballpoint pen developed

1977
First personal computer

1981
Internet opened to the public

When were the first transistor radios?

The first small, portable radios went on sale in 1954, thanks to the invention of the transistor. Tiny transistors were able to make sound signals louder and quickly replaced the large glass valves of early radios. Transistor radios could also work with small batteries as the electric circuit needed less power.

Radio signals are made louder by a transistor.

Battery power makes radios light and portable.

ABOVE A tuning control on the transistor radio selects a radio station. Each station broadcasts its programs on a different radio wavelength.

BELOW Digital radios have a small screen that can display information about the program on air.

Why was digital radio invented?

Digital radio broadcasts first began in 1995 to provide listeners with a wider choice of programs, better sound quality, and more program information. The latest digital radios let listeners pause, rewind, and record live programs. Digital radio works by turning sound and text data into digital signals. The signals are transmitted as radio waves and picked up by digital radio receivers. These have the software to decode and turn the signals back into sound and text.

Radio waves broadcast from a transmitter are picked up by an antenna.

185

COMMUNICATIONS KEY DATES

AD 150	AD 500	1450	1660	1844
Paper first invented	Quill pens used with ink	First printing press	First postal service introduced	Electric telegraph in use

COMPUTERS

ABOVE The world's first successful electronic computer, called ENIAC, was used to make scientific calculations for the US Army.

Who invented the computer?

The English mathematician Charles Babbage invented a steam-powered mechanical computer in 1822. However, neither the technology nor funding existed at that time to build his calculating machine. In 1946, the first fully programmable electronic computer was built by John Eckert and John Mauchly in the US. This enormous, automatic calculating machine filled a room at the University of Pennsylvania.

DID YOU KNOW?
The fastest, most powerful, computers in the world are called supercomputers. In just one second, they can make calculations that a calculator would take 10 years to do.

BELOW *Apple II* personal computer

When was the first PC built?

The first personal computers, or PCs for short, were developed in the 1970s. The Americans Steve Jobs and Steve Wozniak invented the first successful PC for home use in 1977. Their electronic *Apple II* computer had a color screen and keyboard built into one box. Today's PCs can be programmed to do a vast number of different jobs, from word processing or working out calculations to operating computer games.

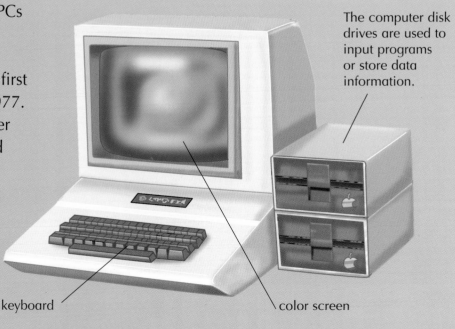

The computer disk drives are used to input programs or store data information.

keyboard

color screen

BELOW The hard-disk unit houses the important electronic components that run the computer, including the disk drives, CPU and RAM.

a CPU computer chip

RAM memory

How do computers work?

Electronic computers work at high speed processing data in the form of text, numbers, pictures, or sounds. They complete their tasks by following the instructions of software programs, which can be loaded onto the machine. The heart of a computer is the hard-disk unit. This contains the central processing unit, or CPU, which controls all of the operations of the PC. The CPU is a microprocessor—a small chip of silicon containing several electronic circuits. The data is stored and retrieved using memory chips called RAM.

What are laptops?

Laptops are small, portable, battery-powered computers. They were invented in 1982 so that business people could use their computers away from the office, for instance, while traveling on a plane, or working from home. Laptops have the same parts and capabilities as PCs, but they are usually small enough to fit in a briefcase. They have a folding case with a built-in keyboard and screen. A touch-pad controls the cursor, rather than an external mouse.

RIGHT Laptop computers are small and light enough to carry anywhere.

touch pad

187

COMMUNICATIONS KEY DATES

AD 150	AD 500	1450	1660	1844
Paper first invented	Quill pens used with ink	First printing press	First postal service introduced	Electric telegraph in use

MAIL

The British Penny Black was the world's first gummed postage stamp. The stamp featured a portrait of the reigning Queen Victoria.

Where was the first postal service?

In 1660, the first official postal service was introduced in England. The Royal Mail was so called because it was mainly used for royal and government letters. Postal charges were based on distance and letters were paid for on delivery. Prepaid postage stamps were first invented in 1840 by the Englishman Rowland Hill. Each stamp cost one penny and paid for the delivery of a letter to anywhere in Britain.

DID YOU KNOW?
Faxes and emails are so much faster at sending letters that ordinary postal services have become known as "snail mail"!

When were postcards invented?

The first postcards were invented in the US by John P. Charlton and printed by the stationer Hyman L. Lipman in around 1861. These were plain cards with just a simple border pattern. By 1873, prestamped plain postal cards were on widespread sale throughout Europe and the US. Picture postcards were developed during the 1890s. They remained a popular way of sending messages up until the start of World War I.

ABOVE In 1902, Britain was the first country to introduce postcards with a full picture on the front. The back was used for the message and the address.

RIGHT Faxes can be sent or received by a fax machine.

Documents are fed into the machine for scanning.

Fax messages are sent using the telephone.

What is a fax machine?

Facsimile, or fax, machines were first used in the late 1980s as a fast way of sending people letters, documents, and pictures electronically. A fax machine works by scanning the image of a document. It measures the areas of light and dark at thousands of different points on the page. This information is turned into electrical signals, which are transmitted down a telephone line to the receiving machine. This machine produces a copy of the original document by printing dark areas of the page as thousands of tiny dots.

BELOW The same email message can be sent to many people at the same time using the Internet. It is also possible to attach photos, music, and video clips to a text message.

Who invented email?

In 1971, the American computer programmer Ray Tomlinson invented electronic mail, called email for short. Tomlinson was working on a program that allowed several users on a single computer to forward text messages to each other, when he realized his invention could also help different computers to communicate. Email means people can send and receive messages quickly and cheaply using computers connected to the Internet—a worldwide network of computers linked by the telephone system. Today, it's possible to send an email to anyone with an email address, anywhere in the world.

189

COMMUNICATIONS KEY DATES

AD 150	AD 500	1450	1660	1844
Paper first invented	Quill pens used with ink	First printing press	First postal service introduced	Electric telegraph in use

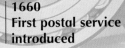

INTERNET

When was the Internet first in use?

The Internet computer network was first opened for public use at universities and colleges in 1981. The network was started in the 1960s by the US Department of Defense, which wanted to set up a new form of communication between its large computers. Today, the Internet links millions of computers all around the world, enabling people everywhere to communicate and exchange information.

LEFT Internet cafés enable people to access information from around the world in seconds.

LEFT Text messages, sound, and even video can be sent via the Internet to an email address across the world in just a few seconds.

How does the Internet work?

Personal computers connect to the Internet using a modem. This device changes text, pictures, sound, and video data into an electrical signal. The signal is sent down a telephone line, or a special cable, to the powerful computer of an Internet service provider. From here, the signal is passed on to other linked computers across the Internet, until it reaches its destination address. The modem connected to the receiving computer changes the electrical signal back into the original data. This is then displayed on the computer screen.

Internet service provider

1876
First telephone invented

1896
First radio transmitter

1938
Ballpoint pen developed

1977
First personal computer

1981
Internet opened to the public

Who invented the World Wide Web?

The British computer scientist Timothy Berners-Lee invented the World Wide Web in 1989. The World Wide Web is a collection of billions of information files or pages. These are held on the computers of colleges, museums, governments, businesses, and individuals around the world. Berners-Lee developed software as a way of linking all this information together on the Internet. By using web browser software on a computer connected to the Internet, it is possible to search the World Wide Web and view specific pages of interest by typing in the website address (www.).

LEFT Fiber optic cable, made from flexible glass, carries light signals at high speed.

DID YOU KNOW?
Most data sent by computers, and other forms of communication, travel at high speed as pulses of laser light. These pass along optical fibers—strands of glass as thin as a human hair!

What is broadband Internet access?

Computers that link to the Internet using a broadband connection can access the World Wide Web faster than ever before. Broadband uses a high-speed cable modem and fiber-optic cable networks. It transmits and downloads data such as email and web pages much faster than dial-up modems using a standard telephone line. Broadband carries larger amounts of data at the same time. This makes it easier to download large information files, such as games, video or music.

RIGHT Large data files are received quickly using broadband.

191

ENTERTAINMENT

Games and toys are invented for our amusement. Discover how guitars make music, how a compact disk player works, and who invented mp3 players. Learn about the photo that took eight hours to produce and how 3-D movie theaters make images leap out of the screen at us. Find out about the changes from early black-and-white television to DVD machines that can even pause live-action scenes.

ENTERTAINMENT KEY DATES

4000 BC	1000 BC	AD 1700	1827	1878
Board game Senet invented	Yoyos popular in Greece	First piano constructed	First photograph is taken	Edison's phonograph plays recorded sound

MUSICAL INSTRUMENTS

How does a piano work?

A piano is a keyboard instrument with a row of black and white keys. When you press a key, a felt-covered hammer hits one or more strings inside. As the strings vibrate, they produce a note. When you take your finger off the key, a part called a damper stops the strings from vibrating. The piano was invented in 1700 by Bartolomeo Cristofori di Francesco, an Italian musical instrument maker.

RIGHT The strings of a modern grand piano are stretched horizontally across a metal frame.

string

hammer

key

damper

soundboard

tuning pegs

frets

strings

bridge

LEFT Instead of a hollow sounding board, an electric guitar has a magnetic "pickup" that turns a string's vibration into an electrical signal, which is then changed into sound by an amplifier.

When was the guitar invented?

In the late 1830s, the Spanish guitar maker Antonio de Torres realized that the shape of the sound board and the size of the hollow body could improve the guitar's sound. To prove it, he made a guitar with a thin arched wooden top and papier mâché back and sides.

1895
Lumiere Brothers
show the first film

1902
Teddy Bear named
after Roosevelt

1925
Logie Baird invents
television

1962
First satellite TV
broadcast

1989
Game Boy
invented

DID YOU KNOW?
The didgeridoo, a wind
instrument invented by the
Aborigines of Australia, can be
as long as 7 feet.

What is a wind instrument?

A wind instrument is a hollow tube that you blow
down to make music. As you blow, air travels
through a mouthpiece or reed and vibrates
inside the tube to produce a note. The
pitch of the note is determined by
the length of the tube and altered
by covering and uncovering
holes in the tube. Woodwind
instruments can be made of
wood, brass, or modern
plastics.

ABOVE Pan pipes are different
lengths of hollow bamboo, each
of which produces a note of a
different pitch when blown.

BELOW The trombone
player changes the pitch
of the note by sliding
a length of tube
in and out.

RIGHT An oboe has a
double reed and holes
which are covered with
the player's fingers.

Who invented the synthesizer?

Canadian Hugh Le Caine built the world's
first successful music synthesizer in 1945.
It was called the Sackbut and it was
built inside a desk. A synthesizer is an
electronic instrument that can imitate
the sounds of musical instruments, as
well as other electronic sounds. A
synthesizer usually has a keyboard
with various controls to select sounds,
vary volume, and add echo or other
sound effects.

LEFT The
latest
keyboards
make all kinds
of sounds and
some can even
generate sound
effects in reaction to
movement.

ENTERTAINMENT KEY DATES

4000 BC	1000 BC	AD 1700	1827	1878
Board game Senet invented	Yoyos popular in Greece	First piano constructed	First photograph is taken	Edison's phonograph plays recorded sound

MUSIC PLAYERS

Who invented the first record player?

The American Thomas Alva Edison built the first record player—the phonograph—in 1878. He was the first person ever to be able to record and play back his sounds. Edison found a way of recording sound onto a moving cylinder wrapped in tinfoil. Sounds caused vibrations that made a stylus (needle) scratch grooves in the cylinder. The sounds would play back when the cylinder was turned again.

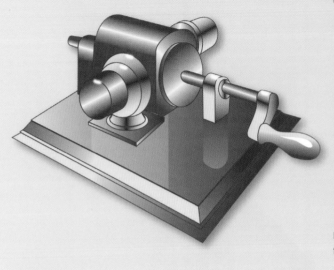

LEFT Edison's phonograph was an instant success, but the tinfoil cylinders wore out quickly.

When were records invented?

In 1888 German-born Emile Berliner invented the gramophone, a music player that used a flat disk to record and play sounds. You turned a handle to turn and play the disk, but these recordings played for just two minutes. In 1948 the long-playing record, or LP, was invented and at last record players could play long pieces of music.

BELOW Sounds are carved into the plastic record in one long spiral from the outside of the record to the center.

ABOVE A stylus (needle) rests in the groove. As the record turns, the stylus vibrates, varying an electrical current that controlled the loudspeaker.

RIGHT These records are "singles"—each side contains just one short piece of music.

1895
Lumiere Brothers
show the first film

1902
Teddy Bear named
after Roosevelt

1925
Logie Baird invents
television

1962
First satellite TV
broadcast

1989
Game Boy
invented

DID YOU KNOW?
When the Sony
Walkman went on sale
in 1979 it was the first
stereo cassette tape
player that was small
enough to carry
around.

How does a compact disc player work?

Unlike records, digital recordings don't store
sound as a continuous streaming signal. A CD is
made up of a series of pits separated by flat areas
called lands. When a laser beam scans the CD
and sees a change from a pit to a land, or from a
land to a pit, it produces the number 1. When it
finds no change, it produces a 0. The CD player
changes this sequence of 0s and 1s back into an
electric current and then back into sound.

What is an MP3 player?

An MP3 player is a small portable
music player that stores your music as
digital information on a hard drive.
The data is compressed—recorded
in a sort of shorthand so that it takes
up much less space on the disk. This
means that the player can store hours
of music. You can load music from
CDs or the Internet onto a computer
and transfer it to your MP3 player.
The MP3 player has a screen from
which you can select an album or
playlist stored on the MP3 player to
play back through your headphones.
German research scientist Karlheinz
Brandenburg invented the MP3
format in 1987.

BELOW The iPod, developed
by Apple, can play music
stored in lots of different
digital formats.

BELOW Sounds are recorded
onto the plastic disc from
the center of the disc to the
outside edge.

disc drive

laser beam

LEFT The first
CD player was
developed in 1982.

197

ENTERTAINMENT KEY DATES

4000 BC	1000 BC	AD 1700	1827	1878
Board game	Yoyos popular in	First piano	First photograph is	Edison's phonograph
Senet invented	Greece	constructed	taken	plays recorded sound

CAMERAS

ABOVE A plate camera

Who took the first photo?

Frenchman Joseph Niépce took the first photograph in 1827. He fixed a metal plate coated with light-sensitive chemicals inside a box that let in no light except through a lens at the front. Eight hours later, an image of the view from the room's window had appeared on the plate. Niepce and others developed plates that took quicker photos.

When was the first roll of film invented?

In 1888, the American, George Eastman, made a camera that took photos on a roll of paper film. Using roll film meant that people could take several photos without having to change plates after each one. It also meant that cameras could be smaller. In 1900, Eastman's Kodak company started to sell the first popular small camera, the box Brownie, for $1.

RIGHT Kodak's motto was "You push the button and we do the rest."

DID YOU KNOW?
The "camera obscura", invented in 16th century Italy, was a darkened room with a small hole that projected the scenery outside onto a wall.

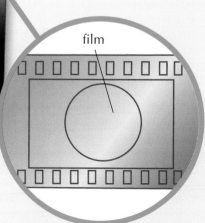

film

press to take a photo

camera settings

What is an SLR camera?

Invented in 1935, the SLR camera lets photographers see an accurate view of what their photo will look like through the lens. In other film cameras, the view through the viewfinder is slightly different from that seen through the lens. When you take a photo using an SLR, a mirror flips up to let light from the lens hit the film rather than go into the viewfinder.

BELOW A CMOS imagesensing microchip turns light into electrical signals in a digital camera.

Pushing a button opens a small window, called the shutter, for a split second to let light hit the film.

Twisting the lens focuses to make sure you get a clear picture. Some SLR cameras have automatic focus.

Inside an SLR camera

CMOS

How does a digital camera work?

Digital cameras, invented in 1988, have a light sensor instead of film. The sensor is a screen divided into tiny squares called pixels. Pixels measure the different colors of light making up an image and a computer chip converts this into a sequence of numbers. Images are stored in memory space inside a camera and also on removable memory cards.

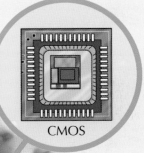

ENTERTAINMENT KEY DATES

4000 BC	1000 BC	AD 1700	1827	1878
Board game Senet invented	Yoyos popular in Greece	First piano constructed	First photograph is taken	Edison's phonograph plays recorded sound

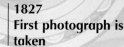

CINEMA

Who invented cinema?

Most people agree that Auguste and Louis Lumière of Lyon, France, invented cinema. In December 1895, they showed moving pictures of factory workers to an audience. The Lumière brothers invented the cinematographe which took lots of photos in a sequence on a long roll of celluloid film. They projected the film onto a wall by shining light through it as they wound the film.

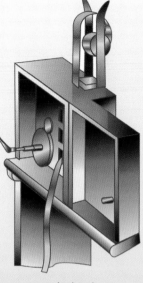

ABOVE A light shone through the images as they passed the lens.

DID YOU KNOW?
Toy Story, released in 1995, was the first full-length computer animated movie. Special computer graphic programs produced most of the images of toy cowboy Woody and spaceman Buzz Lightyear.

When were sound movies first made?

The first short sound movies were made in 1923 by Phonofilm. A new process could record sound onto a strip along the edge of film the so sound and image were always synchronized together. Before then, the only sound in movie theaters was from musicians, such as piano players, who played along with a film in the movie theater. *The Jazz Singer* of 1927 was the first successful talkie, or film with speaking actors.

LEFT A camera and microphne record sound and images simultaneously.

image from film

Optical sound track follows the picture

How do moving pictures work?

Moving pictures work because of a trick of the eye. Each image or frame in a film sequence shows the same objects in slightly different positions. When the sequence is played fast enough, the objects appear to move. The film is fed through a projector that shines a light through the film and projects it onto a white surface where the image appears larger.

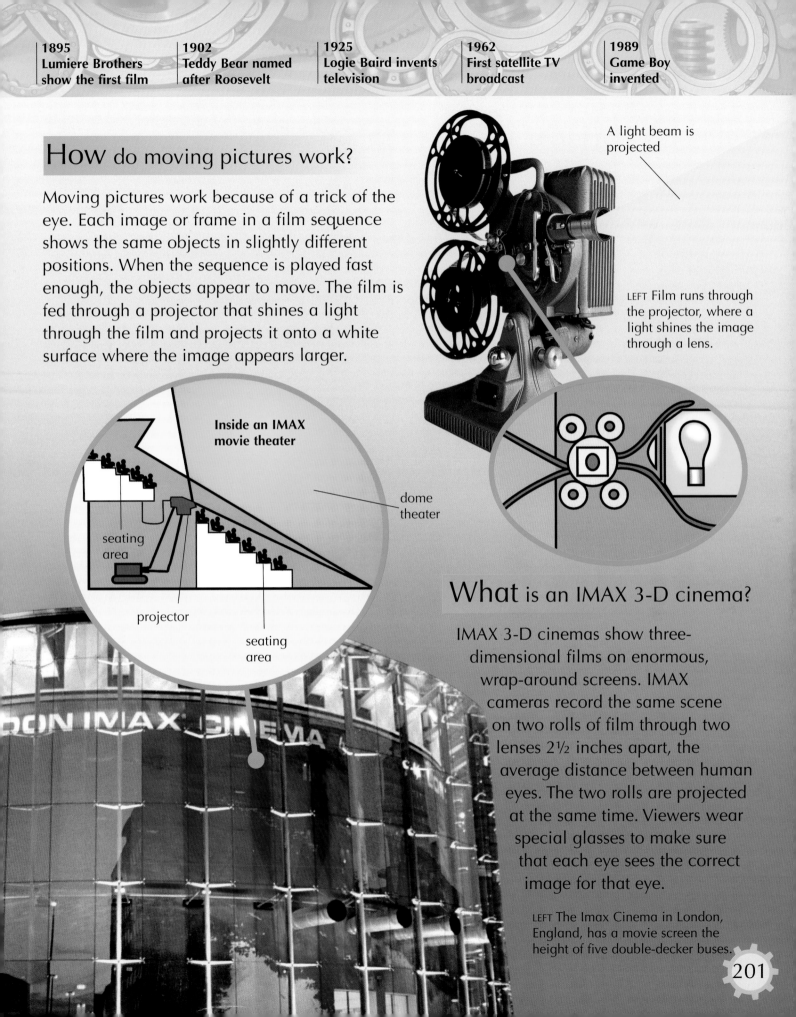

A light beam is projected

LEFT Film runs through the projector, where a light shines the image through a lens.

Inside an IMAX movie theater

dome theater

seating area

projector

seating area

What is an IMAX 3-D cinema?

IMAX 3-D cinemas show three-dimensional films on enormous, wrap-around screens. IMAX cameras record the same scene on two rolls of film through two lenses 2½ inches apart, the average distance between human eyes. The two rolls are projected at the same time. Viewers wear special glasses to make sure that each eye sees the correct image for that eye.

LEFT The Imax Cinema in London, England, has a movie screen the height of five double-decker buses.

201

ENTERTAINMENT KEY DATES

| 4000 BC Board game Senet invented | 1000 BC Yoyos popular in Greece | AD 1700 First piano constructed | 1827 First photograph is taken | 1878 Edison's phonograph plays recorded sound |

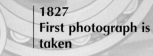

TELEVISION

Who invented television?

In 1925 Scottish inventor, John Logie Baird, transmitted the first recognizable television image. Unfortunately, his mechanical television gave people headaches. Russian-born engineer Isaac Shoenberg came up with a better electronic system in 1936. But it was fellow Russian, Vladimir Zworykin, who added a cathode ray tube to create as well as display pictures.

LEFT Logie Baird's first television.

Where were the first television broadcasts made?

The BBC started regular broadcasts of TV programs in 1936 from London, England. TV cameras converted each second of movement and sound into electrical signals. Aerial transmitters made the signals stronger so they could travel long distances through the air. TV antennas detected the signals and the cathode ray tube converted them into moving pictures on TV screens.

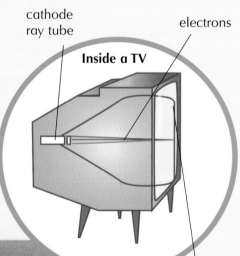

cathode ray tube

electrons

Inside a TV

phosphor-coated screen

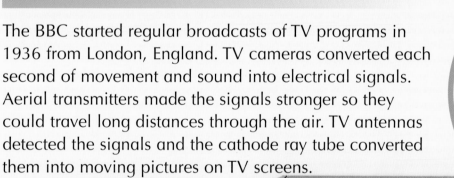

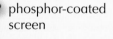

ABOVE In the cathode ray tube, beams of electrons strike phosphors that coat the inside of the screen. The phosphors glow to make the picture.

ABOVE Television program being broadcast from a studio in the 1960s.

ABOVE TV pictures were in black and white until the 1960s.

Satellite in space.

Programsent from studio to satellite.

Satellite dish on your house receives the images from the satellite.

When was satellite TV first broadcast?

The first satellite TV broadcast in July 1962 used communications satellite Telstar 1 to send images of the American flag across the Atlantic Ocean. For satellite TV, a transmitter on Earth broadcasts signals into space. The satellite bounces back scattered signals to different parts of the Earth, where they are collected using satellite dishes connected to TVs.

A digibox converts signals arriving via cable or satellite into a TV picture.

What is digital television?

Digital TV uses digital signals that often produce sharper pictures and better sound than traditional analog signals. Digital signals can carry many more channels, as well as extras such as program information. Programs can be interactive, for example viewers can take part in quizzes, or pay for extra programs using the TV.

DID YOU KNOW?
The biggest flat panel TVs are far lighter than cathode ray tubes and so thin they can be mounted on the wall like a picture.

A remote control uses an infrared beam to change the TV settings.

203

ENTERTAINMENT KEY DATES

4000 BC	1000 BC	AD 1700	1827	1878
Board game Senet invented	Yoyos popular in Greece	First piano constructed	First photograph is taken	Edison's phonograph plays recorded sound

VIDEO AND DVD

Who invented the video recorder?

The Ampex company developed the video recorder in 1956. It was designed for television companies to record programs so they could broadcast them later or more thatn once. Ampex machines recorded TV signals as magnetic patterns on reels of 2-inch wide plastic tape. They were too expensive for most people—a single reel of tape cost the equivalent of 2,000 US dollars today.

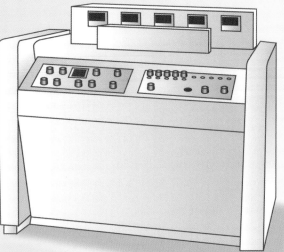

ABOVE The Ampex VTR recorder was revealed for the first time in Chicago on April 14, 1956.

RIGHT Video cassettes were a lot bulkier than CDs or DVDs as information was stored on one long length of magnetic tape.

audio head

magnetic tape

spool

spool

ABOVE The tape winds from one spool to the other through an audio head.

DID YOU KNOW?
DVRs can store video on a computer hard disk without the need for VHS or DVDs. They can even pause live TV shows and instantly replay interesting scenes.

When were VCRs first made for home use?

Sony made the first video recorder for home use in 1964. Its tape could not be changed easily, so the machine could not record much. In 1971, Philips introduced the videocassette recorder, or VCR, which used removable videotape cassettes containing tape. Different companies made different VCR systems but in 1978 JVC produced the standard VHS that became standard worldwide.

Who invented the first camcorder?

The world's first portable camcorder for home use, combining video camera and VCR in one unit, was released by Sony in 1983. The Betamovie was so big and heavy it had to be supported on your shoulder. The next decade was the era of home movies. Camcorders and video cassettes got smaller and had better quality zoom lenses and digital sensors.

The image can be viewed while you are filming and played back right after.

ABOVE Today, camcorders are small and lightweight.

The bumps on the surface of a DVD are read by an infrared laser beam.

LEFT A series of layers or microscopic plastic bumps are created on one side of a DVD.

BELOW DVDs first went on sale in Japan in 1996.

LEFT DVDs can store from 4.5 to 17 gigabytes of information.

What is a DVD?

A DVD is a digital video disc. Developed in the late 1990s, DVD has replaced VHS as the most popular format for playback of pre-recorded video, not only on TVs but also on computers. DVDs have menus so you can jump straight to a scene, watch special features, or select a different language. Since 2005, DVD recorders (DVRs) for home use have become widely available.

ENTERTAINMENT KEY DATES

4000 BC	1000 BC	AD 1700	1827	1878
Board game Senet invented	Yoyos popular in Greece	First piano constructed	First photograph is taken	Edison's phonograph plays recorded sound

TOYS AND GAMES

ABOVE The hoop and stick were popular toys in the 1800s.

Where were the first toys made?

It's likely that the first toys ever made were stone marbles created in ancient Egypt in around 3000 BC. In around 1000 BC people in Greece were playing with stone yoyos. Simple dolls, toys and games were made using stone, wood, ivory and leather. By the 1800s, wind-up toys and music boxes made from tin were popular and porcelain was used to make dolls' heads. Plastic became an important material for toys in the 20th century.

ABOVE
A wind-up monkey

LEFT Marbles are still played today.

RIGHT A musical spinning top

Who invented the teddy bear?

The "Teddy Bear" was invented by Morris Michtom in the US in 1902 and named after American president, Theodore "Teddy" Roosevelt. While on a bear-hunting trip, Roosevelt ordered his men to humanely put a wounded bear out of its misery. In newspaper versions of the story, the bear was drawn as a cute cub, which soon became known as "Teddy's Bear." When Michtom started selling toy replicas of this bear in his store, Roosevelt gave permission for them to be called Teddy bears.

When were were board games first invented?

Board games similar to backgammon, chess, and checkers were being played in ancient cultures such as Babylonia from around 4000 BC. One of the most popular indoor activities for ancient Egyptians was a board game called Senet. The modern board game, Scrabble, was invented in 1931, and Monopoly was created in the US in 1933. Today, many board games include electronic buttons and buzzers instead of pieces that you move by hand.

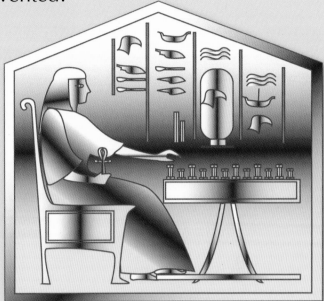

ABOVE Senet was such a popular game in ancient Egypt that it was painted on the tombs of the Pharaohs.

DID YOU KNOW?
The name Lego comes from the Danish "leg godt," meaning play well. Lego bricks were invented in 1949 by Danish toymaker Ole Christiansen.

What are smart toys?

Smart toys are electronic toys that have a computer chip inside them, allowing them to do a variety of clever tricks. Some smart cars can be controlled with a handset or programmed using a computer. There are toy robots that can see, talk and even dance with you, and there are dollhouses with digital characters that interact with each other.

LEFT Robert Adler invented the wireless remote control in 1956.

GREAT INVENTORS

Here is an alphabetical listing of the inventors mentioned in this book and a short biography to tell you something about their lives and what inspired them to produce amazing inventions.

King ALFRED
(849–899, English, p. 151)
"Alfred the Great," king of England, founded the English navy as well as inventing a candle clock in AD 890.

ARCHIMEDES
(287 BC–212 BC, Greek, p. 23)
There is a story of Archimedes leaping out of a bath crying "Eureka!" ('I have found it!'). He realized he could prove a crown was not pure gold using the principle of displacement. He put the crown in water, marked the rise in the water, then did the same with a lump of gold of the same weight. The water rose to a lower level. The gold in the crown must have been mixed with another metal.

Richard ARKWRIGHT
(1732–1792, English, p. 63)
Richard Arkwright, a wigmaker, did not learn to read until he was middle-aged. The cotton spinning and weaving machines he invented made his hometown of Lancashire the center of the world's cotton industry.

Charles BABBAGE
(1792–1871, English, p. 186)
Charles Babbage was a mathematician who spent most of his life creating an "Analytical Engine" that was a mechanical calculating machine. Sadly, his project was never completed, but it earned him the title "grandfather of the modern computer" because his ideas led to the computers we use today.

Leo BAEKELAND
(1863–1944, Belgian, p. 64)
Leo Baekeland knew he could make his fortune if he could come up with an artificial and cheap plastic. He worked for years in a laboratory in a converted barn with his assistant to come up with "Bakelite."

Alexander BAIN
(1811–1877, Scottish, p. 153)
Alexander Bain was at the bottom of his class at school, but from his fascination with clocks and inspiration from a science lecture he saw at the age of 12, he became a great inventor of electrical clocks and telegraph equipment.

John Logie BAIRD
(1888–1946, Scottish, p. 202)
John Logie Baird tried inventing many things, most of which failed, before he set about inventing the first television set. The first set was made from scrap items such as cookie tins and held together with string. He also gave the first demonstrations of stereo sound and color television.

Trevor BAYLIS
(1937–, English, p. 184)
Trevor Baylis invented his wind-up radio after watching a TV program about people in Africa who could not be hear about the spread of AIDS over the radio because they couldn't afford batteries or electricity.

Alexandre-Edmond BECQUEREL
(1820–1891, French, p. 57)
Alexandre-Edmond Becquerel discovered photovoltaic cells for using solar power, through his interest in X-rays, which also led to his most important discovery —radioactivity.

Alexander Graham BELL
(1847–1922, Scottish, p. 182)
Alexander Graham Bell's interest in speech and hearing helped him invent the phone. His first attempts included making a harmonic telegraph in which messages were sent as musical notes. He used some of the money he made from the success of the telephone to open a school to train teachers of the deaf.

Karl BENZ
(1844–1929, German, p. 74)
At first, the public was not interested in Karl Benz's three-wheeled car invention but after Benz, his wife, and two sons drove it 60 miles in one night, the public was hooked and the car industry began. Benz's name lives on in the car industry in

Mercedes-Benz vehicles made today.

Emile BERLINER
(1851–1929, German-born American, p. 196)
Emile Berliner worked for the Bell telephone company. He went on to do his own research into finding a way to record sound. He developed the microphone, the flat recording disk, and the gramophone player.

Timothy BERNERS-LEE
(1955–, English, p. 191)
Timothy Berners-Lee's parents were great mathematicians who helped to develop one of the earliest computers. He went on to set up the World Wide Web, which transformed the Internet into an easy way for everyone to communicate worldwide.

Jeff BEZOS
(1964–, American, p. 173)
As a child, Jeff Bezos converted his parents' garage into a laboratory for his projects. As a young adult he started Amazon, the world's first Internet store.

Clarence BIRDSEYE
(1886–1956, American, p. 29)
In 1912, while Clarence Birdseye was traveling in Canada, he noticed local people freezing freshly caught fish in barrels of icy seawater. When thawed and eaten months later they still tasted fresh. He formed his own company, Birdseye Seafoods Inc., in 1922, and by 1930, was selling 26 different frozen goods.

Georg and Ladislao BIRO
(1900–1985, Hungarian, p. 179)
Journalist Ladislao Biro came up with the idea for a ballpoint pen when he saw quick-drying ink being used at a newspaper printing press. He developed the idea with his brother Georg, a chemist. The brothers gave their name to the biro pen.

Cecil BOOTH
(1871–1955, English, p. 168)
Cecil Booth invented the vacuum cleaner in 1901 and, in 1902, used it to clean ceremonial carpet beneath the thrones for the coronation of King Edward VII.

Karlheinz BRANDENBURG
(1954–, German, p. 197)
Karlheinz Brandenburg studied mathematics and electrical engineering in college. The research he did at university led to his invention of the MP3 player.

Wernher von BRAUN
(1912–1977, German, p. 102)
Wernher von Braun's interest in rockets began as a teenager reading science fiction books. During World War II, he developed the V-2, a huge rocket designed to carry bombs. After the war, von Braun built space rockets in the US.

Isambard Kingdom BRUNEL
(1806–1859, British, p. 66)
Isambard Brunel was an engineer who designed many great ships, railroads and bridges. His first bridge was the Clifton Suspension Bridge, in Bristol, England, built in 1830.

He also built the first steamship to cross the Atlantic, the *Great Western*, launched in 1838. His vast iron ship, the *Great Britain*, built in 1843, was the forerunner of modern ocean-going ships.

Ole CHRISTIANSEN
(1891–1958, Danish, p. 207)
Ole Christiansen was a carpenter who hand-made wooden toys. In 1949 Lego bricks were invented. His company's name, LEGO, combined two Danish words "Leg godt" meaning "play well."

Sir Christopher Sydney COCKERELL
(1910–1999, English, p. 79)
In Sir Christopher Cockerell's first attempts at designing a hovercraft he placed a cat-food can inside a coffee can and blew air from a vacuum cleaner into the space between the two.

L. O. COLVIN
(dates unknown, American, p. 20)
Colvin's milking machine was extremely successful, although the constant suction harmed the cows' udders.

Martin COOPER
(1928–, American, p. 183)
Martin Cooper invented the cell phone. The first call he made as he walked along the streets of New York City was to a land-line telephone belonging to a researcher at a rival company.

Bartolomeo CRISTOFORI
(1655–1731, Italian, p. 194)
Bartolomeo Cristofori worked on his invention, the piano, while caring for the collection of

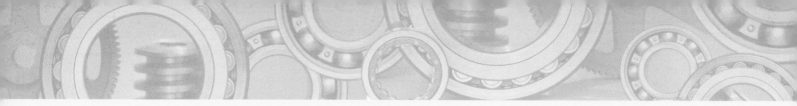

musical instruments belonging to an Italian prince.

Bell CROMPTON
(1845–1939, English, p. 163)
In addition to inventing the electric radiator with Herbert Dowsing, Bell Crompton was behind one of the world's first public lighting programs.

Leonardo DA VINCI
(1452–1519, Italian, p. 11)
Leonardo da Vinci was a great painter, scientist, and inventor. He invented weapons, was one of the first people to dissect and understand how the human body works, how to divert rivers and build canals, and suggested that the Earth went around the Sun at a time when most people believed the Sun circled the Earth.

Gottlieb DAIMLER
(1834–1900, German, p. 73)
By studying the work of other engineers, Gottlieb Daimler was able to devise the first engine to run on gasoline. He went on to build the world's first petrol-driven motorcycle.

George DE MESTRAL
(1907–1990, Swiss, p. 175)
Inventor George de Mestral designed and patented a toy airplane when he was aged 12. As an adult, his invention of Velcro, made him a multimillionaire.

Horace DE SAUSSURE
(1740–1799, Swiss, p. 56)
Horace de Saussure was a mountaineer who discovered 15 minerals, improved

the thermometer and the anemometer, before later inventing the first solar oven.

Antonio DE TORRES
(1817–1892, Spanish, p. 194)
Antonio de Torres learned to make guitars at the age of 33. He went on to design the shape and construction of the modern classical guitar. But he lived in poverty all his life.

John DEERE
(1804–1886, American, p. 17)
John Deere was a blacksmith who invented the steel plow after seeing that cast-iron plows did not work well in the tough prairie soil where he lived.

Herbert DOWSING
(dates unknown, English, p. 163)
Herbert Dowsing was a partner to Bell Crompton and a man of many talents who was a pioneer in the electrical, mechanical, and scientific industries.

Cornelius DREBBEL
(1572–1633, Dutch, p. 128)
Cornelius Drebbel, inventor at the court of James I of Great Britain, left no notes or pictures of his most famous invention —the world's first submarine.

John DUNLOP
(1840–1921, Scottish, p. 72)
John Dunlop thought of his invention, the pneumatic tire, when his young son was advised to cycle to cure a bad cold, and Dunlop made the boy's tricycle more comfortable by equipping it with inflated tubes.

Peter DURAND
(c.1810, English, p. 29)
In 1810, Peter Durand was granted a patent for his tin can for preserving food. His invention saved many soldiers and explorers from starvation.

George EASTMAN
(1854–1932, American, p. 198)
George Eastman was an avid photographer when he was young. His desire to make photography simpler and easier for ordinary people led to the invention of the first Kodak camera.

John ECKERT
(1919–1995, American, p. 186)
John Eckert's and John Mauchly's computer ENIAC was 1,000 times faster than other calculators at the time. Designed for US military calculations, it was a vital tool for scientists working on the first hydrogen bomb.

Thomas Alva EDISON
(1847–1931, American, p. 53, 196)
By the time Thomas Edison was 10 years old he had made his own laboratory at home. Later he set up his own company, called his "invention factory," and went on to invent the phonograph, the electric lightbulb and a microphone to go inside a telephone receiver.

Albert EINSTEIN
(1879–1955, German, p. 11)
Albert Einstein made many new scientific theories, one of which was that a tiny amount of matter, such as an atom, contains a huge amount of

energy. He discovered the mathematical formula that describes how much energy a piece of matter can be changed into, which scientists used as the key to unlock nuclear energy.

Rune ELMQVIST
(1906–1996, Swedish, p. 142)
Rune Elmqvist trained as a doctor before he became an inventor. He developed the first ECG printer to record the heartbeat, as well as the first implantable heart pacemaker.

Gabriel FAHRENHEIT
(1686–1736, German, p. 132)
Gabriel Fahrenheit developed the range of temperatures for his precise thermometers using the coldest temperature he could reach at that time as 0°F and the body temperature of a healthy horse as 100°F.

Michael FARADAY
(1791–1867, English, p. 52)
Michael Faraday knew that a magnet hanging on a thread spins when put near a coil of wire attached to a battery. So in 1831 he tried the opposite. He moved a magnet through a loop of copper wire and generated an electric current through the wire. This was the first electric generator.

Reginald FESSENDEN
(1866–1932, Canadian, p. 184)
Reginald Fessenden was an engineer who was the first person to broadcast using radio waves. His first broadcast was a program of sound and music on Christmas Eve 1906.

Adolf FICK
(1829–1901, German, p. 139)
Adolf Fick tested the first contact lenses he invented on rabbits, then on himself, before trying them out on volunteers.

Alva J. FISHER
(1862–1947, American, p. 164)
Alva Fisher was an engineer based in Chicago, USA, when he patented the washing machine that would make his fortune.

Alexander FLEMING
(1881–1955, Scottish, p. 137)
Alexander Fleming saw how badly soldiers suffered from infections in World War I. So he began to study bacteria in his laboratory. He noticed that mold growing around some of the bacteria was dying off. He obtained a substance from the mold that could kill many different kinds of bacteria. He called it "penicillin."

Henry FORD
(1863–1947, American, p. 66, 74)
Henry Ford, a mechanic, built his first car when he was 30 years old and began the Ford Motor Company in 1903. To keep his cars affordable for everyone, they were built on an assembly line and were only available in one color. He is supposed to have said, "You can have any color you like, so long as it's black."

Enrico FORLANINI
(1848–1930, Italian, p. 79)
Inventor Enrico Forlanini was passionate about designing new vehicles and worked on a variety of helicopters and other aircraft, balloons, and hydrofoils throughout his life

Benjamin FRANKLIN
(1706–1790, American, p. 139)
Benjamin Franklin's curiosity led him to invent many things. But his most famous and risky experiment was when he flew a kite up into a thundercloud to prove that lightning was a giant electrical spark. An electrical spark—like a tiny lightning stroke—jumped from metal to the wet string. He went on to invent the lightning conductor to protect buildings and ships from lightning damage.

John FROEHLICH
(1849–1933, American, p. 18)
John Froehlich was a blacksmith from Iowa. His gasoline-driven tractor was the first one that could be driven forwards and in reverse.

Galileo GALILEI
(1564–1642, Italian, p. 100, 132)
Galileo Galilei invented many things in his lifetime, including the pendulum used to regulate clocks for centuries, an early thermometer, a revolutionary water pump, a military compass that could be used to aim cannonballs accurately, and a special balance that weighed things accurately in either air or water. But his most important achievements were his theories of physics and discoveries about the Earth and the solar system. He built his own telescope and used it to observe the Moon, Sun, planets, and stars.

Henri GIFFARD
(1825–1882, French, p. 83)
Henri Giffard, an engineer, began to experiment with different ways of steering balloons in the 1850s. In 1852, he launched his first controllable airship. The money he earned from this invention funded other projects, such as steam-powered airships.

Robert GODDARD
(1882–1945, American, p. 102)
Robert Goddard loved fireworks. He spent over 20 years experimenting with rockets that continually failed until, in 1926, he created a liquid-fueled rocket that rose high into the air. In his lifetime he was mocked for believing rockets could reach the Moon, but after his death his theories were used to make the rocket that carried the first Americans into space.

Thomas GODFREY
(1704–1749, American, p. 90)
Thomas Godfrey taught himself to read so that he could read books about science and was working as a glazier (installing windows) when he invented the quadrant, a navigational aid.

George H. R. GOSMAN
(dates unknown, American, p. 141)
Captain George Gosman and fellow army officer Lieutenant Albert Rhodes used their own money to build the world's first air ambulance in Fort Barrancas, Florida, in 1910. It crashed on its first test flight.

Johann GUTENBERG
(1400–1468, German, p. 180)
His skill in metalworking helped Gutenberg cast metal letter molds to make a printing press. His best-known publication was the Gutenberg Bible, of which he printed 300 copies.

William HADAWAY
(dates unknown, American, p. 167)
In 1896 William Hadaway was given the first US patent for an electric stove. Later he invented the first electric toaster.

John HADLEY
(1682-1744, English, p. 90)
John Hadley's sextant enabled sailors and explorers to find their positions by measuring how high the Sun or stars were above the horizon.

Otto HAHN
(1879–1968, German, p. 54)
Otto Hahn's discovery, with Lise Meitner, of nuclear fission led to the manufacture of nuclear bombs. But after World War II Hahn became an opponent of nuclear weapons.

James HARGREAVES
(1720–1778, English, p. 62)
Inventors are not always appreciated. Fearful that James Hargreaves' new spinning jenny would leave them without jobs, textile workers broke into his house and smashed his machines.

Sir John HARINGTON
(1561–1612, English, p. 160)
Sir John Harington was a member of Elizabeth I's Royal Court, but like many inventors, was ahead of his time. His ideas for Britain's first flushing toilet were not really taken up by the general public for another 250 years.

John HARRISON
(1693–1796, English, p. 152)
John Harrison was a carpenter who developed his ideas in his spare time, which he spent building and repairing clocks. He eventually became famous for his extremely accurate marine clocks and watches.

John HARWOOD
(1893–1965, English, p. 155)
John Harwood was a watch repairer when he began working on a new, reliable wristwatch with a self-winding mechanism that would fit inside the watch.

Ernst HEINKEL
(1888–1958, German, p. 86)
Ernst Heinkel's fascination with airships led to his interest in aircraft and the development of various planes and even a catapult for launching mail planes from ocean boats.

Peter HENLEIN
(1480–1542, German, p. 154)
Peter Henlein was a locksmith from Nuremburg, Germany, whose invention, the first portable watch, became known as the Nuremburg egg because of its shape.

Joseph HENRY
(1797–1878, American, p. 182)
Joseph Henry was a scientist and inventor whose work in electricity and magnetism

helped bring about the invention of the telegraph, the electric motor, and the telephone.

Rowland HILL
(1795–1879, English, p. 188)
Rowland Hill was a maths teacher when he came up with the idea of the postage stamp. He was later knighted by Queen Victoria for inventing the world's first full postal service.

John P. HOLLAND
(1841–1914, Irish, p. 128)
John Holland moved to the US at the age of 32. He worked, on and off, with the US Navy until he perfected his design for the first truly successful submarine to run above and below water.

Robert HOOKE
(1635–1703, English, p. 134)
Robert Hooke invented the compound microscope. He was so fearful that other scientists would steal his ideas that he often wrote his notes in code.

Edgar Purnell HOOLEY
(1860–date unknown, English, p. 38)
The idea for Edgar Hooley's invention of tarmac came when he noticed a smooth stretch of road that had formed where a barrel of tar had fallen off a cart and was then covered with gravel to reduce the mess.

Christiaan HUYGENS
(1629–1695, Dutch, p. 152, 154)
Christiaan Huygens, a brilliant mathematician from a young age, was also good at making things. In addition to improving the telescope and making a pendulum clock, he suggested that light consists of waves, a

theory that wasn't proved until 150 years later.

Edward JENNER
(1749–1823, English, p. 136)
Edward Jenner was an army surgeon before settling down as a country doctor. His research into viruses led to the invention of vaccinations. His idea was ridiculed at the time and the Church even claimed it was "ungodly" to inject people with animal material.

William le Baron JENNEY
(1832–1907, American, p. 36)
William Jenney designed forts during the Civil War and helped to plan Chicago's rail and road systems before going on to develop the first steel-framed skyscrapers.

Steve JOBS
(1955–, American, p. 186)
Steve Jobs is cofounder of the Apple Computer Company, which began in 1976. He also cofounded Pixar Animation Studios in 1986.

Frederick JONES
(1893–1961, American, p. 71)
Although Frederick Jones is best known for his refrigeration system for trains and trucks, he patented more than 60 other inventions.

Whitcomb JUDSON
(1836–1909, American, p. 174)
When Whitcomb Judson took his "clasp-locker" invention to the World's Fair in 1893, it was ignored. After his death it was remodeled to become the hugely successful zipper.

John KAY
(1704–1780, English, p. 62)
In 1753, John Kay's house was attacked by textile workers who feared his weaving machines would destroy their livelihood. He fled to France, where he died in poverty.

Clarence KEMP
(dates unknown, American, p. 57)
Clarence Kemp sold his first solar water heaters to men whose wives left town for the summer, to save them from having to light up gas boilers themselves. His invention was so popular that within seven years, a third of houses in California had one.

René LAËNNEC
(1781–1826, French, p. 132)
René Laënnec was a doctor who invented a stethoscope to listen to the sounds inside a patient's chest in order to study lung problems. But while studying tuberculosis, he contracted the disease and died aged 45.

Paul LANGEVIN
(1872–1946, French, p. 94)
Paul Langevin was a scientist who studied magnetism. He began exploring the use of ultrasonic sound to detect icebergs after the *Titanic* sank in 1912. It was used to detect submarines during World War I.

Baron Dominique-Jean LARREY
(1766–1842, French, p. 140)
Napoleon described Baron Larrey as "the worthiest man I ever met" for his medical service to wounded soldiers and his

invention of the horse-drawn ambulance.

Hugh LE CAINE
(1914–1977, Canadian, p. 195)
Hugh le Caine studied atomic and nuclear physics and worked on the first radar systems. His lifelong interest in electronic music led him to invent the synthesizer.

Hans LIPPERSHEY
(1570–1619, Dutch, p. 100)
There is a story that spectacle-maker Hans Lippershey's children discovered his "looker" invention (the telescope) while playing with faulty lenses in his workshop.

Joseph LISTER
(1827–1912, English, p. 146)
Surgeon Joseph Lister was inspired to invent methods of sterilization for hospitals because he was horrified by the number of people who died after surgeons operated with unwashed hands.

Auguste and Louis LUMIÈRE
(1862–1954, French, p. 200)
After their photographer father told Auguste about a kinetoscope (a spinning drum that made moving images), the two brothers set about finding a way to project moving images onto a screen and cinema was born.

Tsai LUN
(c. 50–118, Chinese, p. 178)
Tsai Lun got the idea for inventing paper after watching some wasps build their nest by chewing up wood and molding it into thin sheets.

Charles MACINTOSH
(1766–1843, Scottish, p. 174)
One of Charles Macintosh's first inventions was a bleaching powder, and he came up with several other inventions before creating the waterproof fabric that made him famous. Raincoats are still sometimes called "Macintoshes" after him.

Guglielmo MARCONI
(1874–1937, Italian, p. 184)
Guglielmo Marconi read an article suggesting the possibility of using radio waves to communicate without wires. He began experimenting at home. The British Navy was the first to use his radio equipment. His invention later earned him the Nobel Prize in Physics.

John MAUCHLY
(1907–1980, American, p. 186)
After inventing the first electronic digital computer, John Mauchly and his partner John Eckert went on to open the world's first computer company and invent the first computer languages.

Hiram MAXIM
(1840–1916, American, p. 117)
Hiram Maxim's many inventions included an automatic resetting mousetrap, smokeless gunpowder, and a blackboard coating, before his most famous invention—the automatic machine gun.

Wilhelm MAYBACH
(1846–1929, German, p. 73)
Wilhelm Maybach was a skilled engine designer who worked as Gottlieb Daimler's assistant, inventing high-speed internal combustion engines for the first motorcycle.

Frank McNAMARA
(1917–1957, American, p. 170)
Frank McNamara thought his credit card invention would prove to be a passing fad. So he sold his share in the Diners Club card company and never made his fortune.

Gerardus MERCATOR
(1512–1594, Flemish, p. 91)
Gerardus Mercator's mapmaking skills gave him lasting fame—his name was given to a certain type of "projection"—a way of mapping the Earth's curved surface on flat paper.

Morris MICHTOM
(1870–1938, Russian-American, p. 206)
After Morris Michtom invented the teddy bear in 1903, his single store evolved into a huge toy company that continued to sell children's toys until the 1980s.

Etienne and Joseph MONTGOLFIER
(Joseph 1740–1810, Etienne 1745–1799, French, p. 82)
The Mongolfier brothers' first experiment into balloon flight was indoors. They filled an envelope with hot air to make it rise to the ceiling. A year later, they built a hot-air balloon that

carried two people on its first flight.

Samuel MORSE
(1791–1872, American, p. 182)
Samuel Morse was an artist who was inspired to invent the Morse Code after hearing a conversation about electromagnetic devices while traveling on board a ship.

Paul MÜLLER
(1899–1965, Swiss, p. 24)
Scientist Paul Muller worked on synthetic dyes before inventing the insecticide DDT, which played a key role in eradicating the fatal disease malaria in some parts of the world.

William MURDOCH
(1754–1839, English, p. 49)
Sitting by his fire one evening, William Murdoch put some coal dust into his pipe and put it in the fire. Coal gas formed and came out of the pipe shining brightly and Murdoch realized he had invented gas lighting.

Tsuneya NAKAMURA
(dates unknown, Japanese, p. 155)
Tsuneya Nakamura headed a team of engineers working at Seiko for 10 years to develop the first quartz wristwatch to be sold to the public in 1969.

Thomas NEWCOMEN
(1663–1729, English, p. 50)
Thomas Newcomen's steam-powered water pump infringed a patent taken out by Thomas Savery, so he had to make him a partner. The pump was a great success, but Newcomen did not become rich.

Isaac NEWTON
(1642–1727, English, p. 100)
Isaac Newton showed that every piece of matter attracts every other piece by gravity. He explained the movements of the tides, of the Moon around the Earth, and of the planets around the Sun. His work on forces led to the unit of force, the "newton," being named after him. He made huge advances in the study of light, and in 1687 he invented a reflecting telescope.

Joseph NIEPCE
(1765–1833, French, p. 198)
Joseph Niepce worked on a kind of internal combustion engine before experimenting with cameras from 1816. He eventually invented a way of making permanent photographs.

Ransom E. OLDS
(1864–1950, American, p. 66)
Ransom Olds built a three-wheeled steam carriage in 1887, a four-wheeled steam car in 1893, and a gasoline car in 1896. In 1899, he founded the Olds Motor Works, which sold the first "Oldsmobile" car in 1901.

J. Robert OPPENHEIMER
(1904–1967, American, p. 121)
During World War II, Robert Oppenheimer led the US government's project to build an atomic bomb. The first was tested in July 1945, three weeks before A-bombs were dropped on the Japanese cities of Hiroshima and Nagasaki.

Elisha Graves OTIS
(1811–1861, American, p. 37)
Elisha Otis got the idea for an elevator safety break when he was working in a factory in New York City. His first brake was for the hoist used to take heavy objects up to other floors.

Charles PARSONS
(1854–1931, Irish-English, p. 51, 80)
Charles Parsons invented the steam turbine. In 1884, he set up the Parsons Marine Steam Turbine Company to build steam ships. He was knighted in 1911.

Louis PASTEUR
(1822–1895, French, p. 21)
Louis Pasteur was not considered a bright student in school but by the time he was in his twenties he was famous for his scientific experiments. He discovered that bacteria cause disease and invented pasteurization, a means of making milk safe to drink.

James RITTY
(1837–1918, American, p. 172)
James Ritty was a bar owner who invented his cash register, the "Incorruptible," with the help of his brother John, who was a mechanic.

Wilhelm RÖNTGEN
(1845–1923, German, p. 144)
Wilhelm Rontgen was not sure what his discovery was, so named it "X-ray." In 1901 he was given the first ever Nobel Prize for Physics for his discovery.

Ernst RUSKA

(1906–1988, German, p. 135)
Electrical engineer Ernst Ruska built the first "magnetic lens" to bend beams of electrons. He later invented the electron microscope. He was joint winner of the Nobel Prize for Physics in 1986.

Åke SENNING

(1915–2000, Swedish, p. 142)
Senior physician and researcher Åke Senning fitted the world's first heart pacemaker in 1958, with the help of an engineer at a university hospital in Sweden.

James SHARP

(1790–1870, English, p. 167)
James Sharp first installed an experimental gas stove in his home in 1834 and opened a factory to sell versions of his gas stove in 1836.

Percy SHAW

(1890–1976, English, p. 39)
Percy Shaw became rich from his invention of cat's eyes, which he first called "Reflecting Roadstuds." They won him an OBE medal for his contribution to road safety.

Isaac SHOENBERG

(1880–1963, Russian, p. 202)
Isaac Shoenberg persuaded the company he worked for, EMI, to fund a research project on televisions. In 1932, his UK team succeeded in making an electronic television picture-generating tube.

Christopher SHOLES

(1819–1890, American, p. 180)
Christopher Sholes was a newspaper printer who invented a typewriter in 1868. Its design was based on an earlier page-numbering machine he had invented.

Igor SIKORSKY

(1889–1972, Russian, p. 84)
Igor Sikorsky was studying

engineering when he saw a newspaper picture of Orville Wright and his plane. It inspired him to take up aviation instead, and he invented the helicopter in 1939.

John SMEATON

(1724–1792, English, p. 32)
John Smeaton invented an improved form of concrete while building the Eddystone Lighthouse off the coast of South Devon, England. The lighthouse stood for over 100 years before being dismantled and moved onto land at Plymouth.

Percy SPENCER

(1894–1970, American, p. 166)
Percy Spencer, inventor of the microwave oven, was an inquisitive and inventive man who took out over 150 different patents in his lifetime!

Elmer SPERRY

(1860–1930, American, p. 91)
In 1880, Elmer Sperry opened a company to make electric dynamos and arc lamps he had invented as a teenager. He went on to found seven more companies making other

inventions, including the gyrocompass.

John STARLEY

(1854–1901, English, p. 72)
John Starley was the nephew of James Starley, who had invented one of the first high wheeler bicycles. The basic design of John's own "safety" bicycle is still followed today.

George STEPHENSON

(1781–1848, English, p. 76)
George Stephenson taught himself to read and then worked his way up from shoveling coal into steam engines to building and inventing them. His steam engine *Locomotion* pulled the world's first passenger train.

Fritz STRASSMANN

(1902–1980, German, p. 54)
Chemist Fritz Strassman helped discover nuclear fission, which made the use of nuclear power possible.

Gideon SUNDBACK

(1880–1954, Swedish-born Canadian, p. 174)
Gideon Sundback's invention, the zipper, was based on the work of other engineers. A patent was issued for it in 1917 under the name "separable fastener."

Ray TOMLINSON

(1941–, American, p. 189)
When Ray Tomlinson first invented his email messaging system even he did not realize how important it was to become. It was Tomlinson who came up with the "@" symbol.

Anton VAN LEEUWENHOEK

(1632–1723, Dutch, p. 134)

The microscope was considered a toy until Anton van Leeuwenhoek used it to study fibers in his fabric shop. He went on to use his microscope to study living things and was the first person to see blood flowing in the tiny blood vessels we call capillaries.

Alfred VAIL

(1807–1859, American, p. 182)

Alfred Vail was an inventor who helped Samuel Morse develop his telegraph and code.

Hermann VON HELMHOLTZ

(1821–1894, German, p. 138)

Hermann von Helmholtz influenced inventions concerning sound and electromagnetism. He invented an ophthalmoscope for examining the inside of the human eye.

Alessandro VOLTA

(1745–1827, Italian, p. 52)

Alessandro Volta invented the first electric battery in 1800. In 1881, the volt (the basic unit of electrical force) was named after Volta in his honor.

Ezra WARNER

(dates unknown, American, p. 29)

Ezra Warner's can opener, invented in 1858, had a sharp blade to pierce the lid and a saw to cut around it. It was too dangerous for home use so grocers had to open the cans before customers left the store.

Robert Alexander WATSON-WATT

(1892–1973, Scottish, p. 92)

Robert Watson-Watt was a weather forecaster who noticed that thunderstorms caused crackles on a radio. In 1935, he devised a way of reflecting waves off an object such as an airplane to find out how far away and in which direction the aircraft was going. He had invented the first workable system for using radar (Radio Detection And Ranging).

James WATT

(1736–1819, Scottish, p. 50)

James Watt was given a model of Newcomen's steam engine to fix, when he decided he could make a more efficient version. Watt's improved steam engines transformed the coal and textile industries.

Horace WELLS

(1815–1848, American, p. 146)

Horace Wells was a dentist who came up with the idea for anesthetics when he and his wife saw a demonstration of laughing gas being used by a traveling circus.

Robert WHITEHEAD

(1823–1905, English, p. 129)

Robert Whitehead and his son were working on new weapons ideas for warships when they came up with the design for the first self-propelling torpedo in the 1850s.

Frank WHITTLE

(1907–1996, English, p. 86)

Frank Whittle was a pilot who wrote his first papers on jet engines when he was just 21 years old. But a lack of interest from the UK Air Ministry meant he wasn't able to develop the first jet engine for many years. It flew for the first time in 1941.

Steve WOZNIAK

(1950–, American, p. 186)

Steve Wozniak had built his own radio station by the age of 11 and, as a teenager, built a computer in the garage. He went on to become cofounder of Apple Computer Company, with his friend Steve Jobs.

WRIGHT brothers

(Orville 1871–1948, Wilbur 1867–1912, American, p. 86)

The Wright brothers taught themselves all the mechanical skills they needed to set up a bicycle shop. After taking up gliding they decided to build a bicycle with wings and an engine to turn a propeller. They were the first people in history to build a successful airplane.

Vladimir ZWORYKIN

(1889–1982, Russian, p. 202)

Scientist Zworykin invented the cathode ray tube, which displays the picture in a television set. But his feelings about the television set were not positive. He said, "I would never let my own children watch it."

INDEX

ACKNOWLEDGEMENTS

Artwork supplied through the SGA Illustration Agency by Geoff Ball and James Alexander

Photo credits:
b = bottom, t = top, r = right, l = left, m = middle

Cover: t Corbis bl Getty br Corbis

Running head band Photodisc/Getty Images, 1 Comstock, 2 Stockdisc Photos/Getty Images, 3l Photodisc/Getty Images, 3m Brand X Pictures/Jupiter Images, 3r Photodisc/Getty Images, 7 Bettman/Corbis, 8 Bettman/Corbis, 9l Photodisc/Getty Images, 9m Bettman/Corbis, 10 Comstock/Jupiter Images, 10bl Bettman /Corbis, 11 tl Bettman/Corbis, 11tr Bettman/Corbis, 11br Rick Fredman/Corbis, 12mr Rick Friedman/Corbis, 12bl Digital Art/Corbis, 13t Toshiyuki Aizaw/Reuters/Corbis, 13b Reuter/Corbis, 14/15 David Frazier/Corbis, 16 David Frazier/Corbis, 18 Corbis, 19 David Frazier/Corbis, 20 David Frazier/Corbis, 22 Reed Kaestner/Corbis, 23 David Frazier/Corbis, 24/25 Warren Jacobi/Corbis, 26l Richard Gross/Corbis, 26r David Frazier/Corbis, 27 David Frazier/Corbis, 28 Richard Gross/Corbis, 29 David Frazier/Corbis, 30/31 Image Ideas/Index Stock Imagery, Inc., 32 Mick Roesssler/Corbis, 33t Image Ideas/Index Stock Imagery, Inc., 33b Reed Kaestner/Corbis, 34/35 Brand X Pictures/Jupiter Images, 36/37 Image Ideas/Index Stock Imagery, Inc., 38/39 Digital Vision/Getty Images, 40 Digital Vision/Getty Images, 41 Image Ideas/Index Stock Imagery, Inc., 42t Photodisc/Getty Images, 42m Photodisc/Getty Images, 42b Brand X Pictures/Jupiter Images, 44 42b Brand X Pictures/ Jupiter Images, 45lm 42b Brand X Pictures/Jupiter Images, 45r Digital Vision/Getty Images, 47 Photodisc/Getty Images, 48 Brand X Pictures/Jupiter Images, 49 Photodisc/Getty Images, 50 Brand X Pictures/Jupiter Images, 53 Photodisc/Getty Images, 54 Brand X Pictures/Jupiter Images, 56 Photodisc/Getty Images, 58 Photodisc/Getty Images, 60/61 Brand X Pictures/ Jupiter Images, 63l Flat Earth, 63r Brand X Pictures/Jupiter Images, 64 Digital Vision/Getty Images, 65t Brand X Pictures/Jupiter Images, 65b Digital Vision/Getty Images, 67m Photodisc/ Getty Images, 67b Banana Stock/Jupiter Images, 68/69 Brand X Pictures/Jupiter Images, 71m Thinkstock/Jupiter Images, 71b Digital Vision/Getty Images, 73 Flat Earth, 74 Brand X Pictures/Jupiter Images, 75t Brand X Pictures/Jupiter Images, 75m Leo Dennis Productions/Brand /Corbis, 76 Digital Vision/Getty Images, 77 Paul Saunders/Corbis, 78 Brand X Pictures/ Jupiter Images, 79 Ben Blankenburg/Corbis, 80t Brand X Pictures/Jupiter Images, 80b Larry Mulvehill/Corbis, 82 Brand X Pictures/Jupiter Images, 84/85 Brand X Pictures/Jupiter Images, 86 Brand X Pictures/Jupiter Images, 87 Digital Vision/Getty Images, 88 Photodisc/Getty Images, 89l Photodisc/Getty Images, 89m Brand X Pictures/Jupiter Images, 89r Alan Levenson/ Corbis, 91 Digital Vision/Getty Images, 92 Photodisc/Getty Images, 93t Digital Vision/Getty Images, 93b Brand X Pictures/Jupiter Images, 94 Alan Levenson/Corbis, 96/97 J Stephen Hicks/Corbis, 97t Brand X Pictures/Jupiter Images, 98 Photodisc/Getty Images, 99l Photodisc/Getty Images, 99m Photodisc/Getty Images, 99r Photodisc/Getty Images, 101 NASA, 102 NASA, 104 NASA, 105t Photodisc/Getty Images, 106 NASA, 107 Photodisc/Getty Images, 108/109 NASA, 110/111 NASA, 112/113 Brand X Pictures/Jupiter Images, 114 Flat Earth, 115 RubberBall Productions, 116 Thinkstock/Jupiter Images, 117 Brand X Pictures/Jupiter Images, 119 Brand X Pictures/Jupiter Images,, 120/121 Brand X Pictures/Jupiter Images,, 122/123 Brand X Pictures/Jupiter Images, 123t Lushpix/Unlisted Images, Inc., 124 Brand X Pictures/Jupiter Images, 125 Superstock, Inc., 126 Brand X Pictures/Jupiter Images, 127 Lushpix/ Unlisted Images, Inc., 128/129 Brand X Pictures/Jupiter Images, 130/131 Photodisc/Getty Images, 132t Brand X Pictures/Jupiter Images, 132b Photodisc/Getty Images, 133/134 Photodisc/Getty Images, 135 Brand X Pictures/Jupiter Images, 136 Blend Images, LLC, 137t Photodisc/Getty Images, 137b Brand X Pictures/Jupiter Images, 138 Photodisc/Getty Images, 139 Brand X Pictures/Jupiter Images, 140 lr (inset) Photodisc/Getty Images, 140/141 Brand X Pictures/Jupiter Images, 142t Brand X Pictures/Jupiter Images, 142b Photodisc/Getty Images, 143t Brand X Pictures/Jupiter Images, 143b Photodisc/Getty Images, 144 Brand X Pictures/Jupiter Images, 145t Brand X Pictures/Jupiter Images, 145m Allen Bell/Corbis, 145b Photodisc/ Getty Images, 146/147 Brand X Pictures/Jupiter Images, 147t Tim O'Hara/Corbis, 148 Photodisc/Getty Images, 149l Photodisc/Getty Images, 149 m Flat Earth, 149r Photodisc/Getty Images, 150 Flat Earth, 151 Ingram Publishing, 152t Tom Grill/Corbis, 152b Superstock Inc., 153/154 Photodisc/Getty Images, 155/156 Photodisc/Getty Images, 157 Banana Stock/ Jupiter Images, 158 Digital Vision/Getty Images, 159lm Digital Vision/Getty Images, 159r Photodisc/Getty Images, 160 Comstock/Jupiter Images, 161/162 Digital Vision/Getty Images, 163 Comstock/Jupiter Images, 164 Randy Faris/Corbis, 165l Digital Vision/Getty Images, 165r Image Source, 166 Lawrence Manning/Corbis, 167 Randy Faris/Corbis, 168 Comstock/ Jupiter Images, 169t Lawrence Manning/Corbis, 1699b Photodisc/Getty Images, 170 StockDisc/ Corbis, 171t Don Hammond/Design Pics/Corbis, 171m (inset) Image 100/Corbis, 171b Image 100/Corbis, 172 Jack Hollingsworth/Corbis, 173tr Image 100/Corbis, 173tl (inset) Photodisc/Getty Images, 173b Simon Marcus/Corbis, 174t StockDisk/Corbis, 174b Comstock Select/Corbis, 175 Mark Karrass/Corbis, 175 b Ben Blakenburg/Corbis, 176 Photodisc/Getty Images, 177l Digital Vision/Getty Images, 177mr Photodisc/Getty Images, 178 Comstock/ Jupiter Images, 179t Flat Earth, 179b Comstock/Jupiter Images, 180 Comstock/Jupiter Images, 181t Getty Images, 181b StockDisc/Corbis, 182 Comstock/Jupiter Images, 183l (inset) StockDisc/Corbis, 183 Banana Stock/Jupiter Images, 184 Comstock/Corbis, 185t Classic PIO, 185r David Frazier/Corbis, 187tr Reed Kaestner/Corbis. 187 l (inset) Photodisc/Getty Images, 187r (inset) StockDisc/Corbis, 18b Comstock/Jupiter Images, 188 Photodisc/Getty Images, 189t Comstock/Corbis, 189b Tom Grill/Corbis, 190tm Banana Stock/Jupiter Images, 190/191 Bloomimage/Corbis, 191m (inset) Photodisc/Getty Images, 191b Banana Stock/Jupiter Images, 192 Banana Stock/Jupiter Images, 193lm Banana Stock/Jupiter Images, 193r Photodisc/Getty Images, 194/195 Photodisc/Getty Images, 195b Bob Jacobson/Corbis, 196 Comstock/Jupiter Images, 197l Comstock/Jupiter Images, 197r Lushpix/Unlisted Images, Inc., 198 Comstock/Jupiter Images, 199t Comstock/Jupiter Images, 199t Banana Stock/Jupiter Images, 199b Comstock/Jupiter Images, 200/201 ImageState, 201t Comstock/Jupiter Images, 202 Comstock/Jupiter Images, 203t Bloomimage/Corbis, 203b Banana Stock/Jupiter Images, 204 Comstock/Jupiter Images, 205t Banana Stock/Jupiter Images, 205b Comstock/Jupiter Images, 206 Comstock/Jupiter Images, 207 StockDisc/Corbis